I AM a Brilliant Woman

Volume Two:

Stories of women who have found deeper meaning and happiness in their life.

Karen Klassen

Contributing Authors

Paige Stevensen	Jackie Maclean
Dana Harrison	Amy van Meijl
Sandra Catania	Adora Nwofor
Donna Malchuk	Leticia Jones
Elizabeth Bennett	Shauna Walker

Visit

womenembracingbrilliance.com

I AM a Brilliant Woman Volume Two

Editors: Brenda Frame and Sylvia Cole

Formatting by Bojan Kratofil

Cover Design by Okomto (Fiverr)

For inquiries, please contact: Karen Klassen

www.womenembracingbrilliance.com

ISBN: 978-0-9918890-3-7

First Edition

Table of Contents

This book is dedicated to the courageous women who are awakening and reclaiming their feminine power and the men who honour them.

Introduction

Brilliance: radiating a high degree of light.

The path to greater meaning and happiness is what many of us are striving for. What women want most for themselves is to be happy, fulfilled, loved and accepted for who they are.

The journey to happiness is not an easy one. Those who persevere and say "Yes" to overcoming all that stands in their way, are the ones who enjoy a life like no other.

We see the uprise of chaos and crisis in the world, and at the same time we are also seeing more and more people choosing love over fear, contribution over competition and peace over crisis. This is an exciting time for humanity to rise up, to support, encourage, and inspire each other to be the highest version of ourselves.

As we spiral up out of fear, negativity and drama we activate our deepest potential and we consciously become more and more aware that "life" is supporting us. Women are discovering an incredible force within as they embrace their own divine feminine power, their own inner *brilliance.*

What is a brilliant woman? A brilliant woman is a woman who has connected to her *soul.* It is her *soul-force* that once ignited will quantum leap her life from struggle, pain and lack to a life of great love, prosperity and fulfillment. Every woman is born brilliant ~ radiating a high degree of light. Unfortunately, over time this light can diminish as we fall into the sleep of forgetfulness. We are waking up one by one, and I truly believe, that the awakened women will be the ones who shift the consciousness on this planet. It is only a *brilliant* woman who has ignited her own *soul-force* who can then hold space for a man to awaken his inner brilliance.

We have all experienced tragedy, trauma, and loss to one degree or another. As we rise up and remember who we are, we begin to understand that all the pain and suffering we experienced was waking us up to a deeper truth - to love ourselves, to forgive, to be kind, to accept what is and surrender to the moment. We no longer need to learn from crisis in order to see that life is only taking us in one direction - *to love.* As we remember this truth, we find deeper meaning and peace of mind.

As women we're being called to reclaim our feminine power and embrace the "I AM", the two most powerful words in the English language. Any time you start a sentence with *I am,* you are **creating** what you are and what you want to be. You determine your self-worth, as you are the only one who gets to decide on the word that comes next.

I AM a Brilliant Woman is an invitation for women around the world to stand in their power. To unapologetically declare, "I AM a Brilliant Woman" no matter what you have done or experienced.

I believe there is a leader in every woman, whether she wants to lead the world, her community or to lead a fulfilling and meaningful life for herself and her family. As awakened women we have the power to create a new feminine leadership model that can create a beautiful world where we honour and respect men, children, our planet, each other and especially ourselves. A model that includes collaboration, intuition, creativity, vulnerability, humility and empathy.

Over the years I have been blessed to listen to many incredible stories, as women shared their deepest truths and what it took for them to rise up and take a stand for their own self worth. Each of you has a story - an empowered story to be shared. We have a lot to learn from each other. It is time for all of us to listen to our voices, our stories and to be shown a new evolutionary path of possibilities.

This is why I was inspired to create this series of books. A book of bold women who have experienced obstacles and setbacks and yet they are unstoppable in their pursuit to greater happiness.

Accessing our divine feminine power is not a journey we take alone. We need the support and encouragement of our goddess girlfriends, and of bold women on a similar journey. The more we share our stories, the more we realize how much we all have in common and we cease to judge or criticize.

This book is a collaboration of ten extraordinary women, each contributing one chapter based on her beliefs, her life experience, her personality and the gifts she is here to share as a source of inspiration for women.

This book is written by women *for* women who are ready to ignite their own heart's desires. Our intention is to offer inspiration and encouragement that will ignite the reader's heart and empower her to embrace and activate her own *soul-force.*

I believe there is a magical combination of happiness and meaning that can ultimately lead to a life well lived.

In Gratitude,

Karen Klassen

Founder of Women Embracing Brilliance

The Brilliant Woman Declaration

I (your name) make a heart centered commitment that from this moment forward, I will never degrade, gossip, cut down, name call or say mean or spiteful words to or about another woman. She is my sister and is a reflection of who I am. I love myself way too much to speak negatively about others.

And so it is.

I AM Illuminated

Michelle,

You are worth it!

and more!

Paige

From Default by Design

By Paige Stevensen

From challenged beginnings

Marquee lights boldly light up the night sky as throngs of people cling to their tickets, anticipating me speaking on stage. I am famous.

Yes, my imagination brilliantly created a world I could exist in, so I could escape the real world. Most young children do, I know. Why is that? I was no different, but my childhood was.

My parents raised me and my three sisters in a Christian religious cult. Now, I know you may be thinking, *Religious cult*, really?" To me, a cult is something that means you're being told how to act, behave, live, entertain, read, breed, visit, date, marry and socialize - in addition to how often and with whom. It was like everything we did was under the scrutiny of 'big brother'.

Women were not allowed to wear pants, as it was judged to be against the Lord's way. You were not allowed to have Christmas trees or mix with outsider/worldly children. Women and girls had to wear skirts or dresses, and wear their hair either long or in a bun. You were not allowed to cut it. The only jewellery that could be worn was your matrimonial gold wedding band, which could not even contain any diamonds. Makeup of any kind, especially red lipstick was forbidden.

This deeply religious lifestyle taught me what to think, how to behave, what to say and what to do. If I did not follow the rules, I would be punished and abused in unimaginable ways. I learned to completely close off my physical world to escape into the blissful playground of my imagination, with its vivid colors and storylines. I used to love staying in this space, because 'there', I was safe. My imagination connected me to the invisible worlds others could not see.

Up to the age of nine, I was gifted. I could see things that my parents called, "my imaginary friends". I was told to shut them out, as it was not the Lord's way. To me, what I imagined as a child was real. As I got older, I started to believe that my dreams could never be possible. The influence of my parents' limiting beliefs rubbed off on me and blocked my expression of the vibrant, big life I used to escape to in my dreams.

For most of my childhood, I never saw myself as having my own identity. I felt like the forgotten one. My two older sisters and my younger sister appeared to have a connection with our family, while I felt like the outcast. It was my imagination that became my confidant; a space I would slip into whenever I felt troubled.

Both of my parents worked a lot. My dad worked out of town and my mother held two or three jobs at a time, according to her, "*to make ends meet*". I was, in truth, a latchkey kid. The result of this was that I had no supervision before and after school. When my little sister and I would get home from school, we were left to our own choices. I was a chubby girl and had very few friends. My little sister on the other hand, had many friends and would run over to a friend's place to play. I would be left at home by myself. The result: I would resort to food for comfort.

I would eat anything available in the house. I was eating to mask my feelings. Since we were a 'have-not family', the food in our house was generally not healthy.

Most of my childhood was filled with 'scarcity thinking' by my parents. Growing up, I heard, "*we don't have money for that*", "*we're not the Joneses*" and the much revered comment, "*money doesn't grow on trees*".

My little-girl ears never heard my parents say encouraging statements like, "*you can be anything you want to be*", "*anything you choose to be is at your fingertips*", "*go for it*" or "*don't let anybody talk you out of your dreams*". Their views were a mixture of the religious dogma they followed, the poverty thinking they lived and, of course, the individual resentment of, "*this is what life gave me*".

With so many relentless conditions placed upon my young, imaginative mind, it was nearly impossible to think that I would ever be more than the insignificance of what I heard and felt. As a result, I fell into the pattern of closing down emotionally. I dimmed the lights on the imagination that carried me away, long before I had a chance to germinate those dreams and have them flower into reality.

It was during this time that my parents divorced, and since divorce was not allowed in our church, our family was quickly excommunicated from the church and, therefore, from the community.

Depth of conditioning

I never revealed to anybody, the abuse that I had undergone. I went through my adolescence withdrawn and aggravated. I felt abandoned, emotionally distraught and believed that I mattered to nobody. My imagination, which sheltered me through my younger years, became a distant companion. I taught myself to shut that part of me down. The magical experiences that I truly thought existed were apparently not evident to others. I decided that they could no longer be a part of my reality going forward. I had to push aside my past and get serious about my life; yet, without the loving and supportive foundation from my parents, I lacked the core strength, confidence and courage to make the kinds of choices required to pursue my dreams.

My childhood environment taught me to believe that I was to get married, own a house, raise children and find a good job with a pension. By meeting somebody who I thought was smarter than me, had more money than me and had a university education, I thought we would be the perfect mix to have a beautiful life. My security and future were tied to people and events outside of myself and my own abilities.

So, I did just that. I married a man with whom I was truly mesmerized. He was in his thirties, had never had a long-term girlfriend and was extremely focused on his accounting career. His life expanded when he met me. I was a 22-year-old girl who was full of excitement, paying attention to him in a way that he had never experienced before. We thought we had died and gone to heaven. He gave me almost everything I wanted.

What I didn't realize then, was his inability to create closeness with others. He isolated himself socially. This paved the way for a lack of intimacy and excitement in our marriage. Once again, my life was leaving me feeling abandoned and disconnected in the relationship that was most important to me.

I did everything I could to fill the emptiness inside of me by trying to be what I thought this world expected of me. However, in the back of my mind were thoughts reminding me that, "I'm not good enough" or "I will never amount to anything". My life was ruled by the critical chatter of others and a deep sense of commitment to my wedding vows. As my life slipped further and further away from the blissful exodus I had hoped it would be, the depth of the hidden truth took its toll on me.

The last 10 years of my marriage went straight to rock bottom. My husband ended up on a disability pension after being diagnosed with clinical depression and never returned to work. I was thrust into the primary role of being the provider for our family. I was repeating my mother's life.

I held down the jobs of looking after the kids and working as a secretary. As well, I did some part-time direct sales jobs, "*to make ends meet*". I did well with my side businesses and enjoyed both the social rewards of friendships and the validation that came with achieving success. Shortly thereafter, I realized that my success was sadly due to wanting to get away from my home life.

I was so unhappy. At the time, I didn't know that avoiding my life was actually a sign of how much it wasn't working.

For 23 years, I remained married and raised our two children. As I think about it now, it was quite amazing that I never had a desire to have an affair.

Reopening to imagination

For most of my life, I felt God did not exist. My childhood experiences in my parents' religious cult and all the abuse I lived through, left me feeling spiritually abandoned. How could such a being allow all the suffering I had endured? I had chosen to shut out all divine interventions. I had had little value as a girl and had been fed beliefs about life that limited my ability to dream and imagine my potential. I was like a robot going through the motions.

With time, I came to realize that I didn't have to listen to other people. I could think on my own and didn't need anybody telling me what to experience or feel. My 'truth' began stirring deep inside of me. I had been a very sensitive, empathic and intuitive girl – and still am. I had always been able to sense angelic things around me that no one else could see. When I was young, I was told that I was 'different' and that I had learning disabilities because I was often in la-la land.

Imagining a life more aligned with my true being began to emerge after reading one of the most influential books on my journey to awakening. *The Celestine Prophecy* was a looking-glass moment for me, as the story it shared made sense to me. Finally, I was reading something that made me say, "Oh yes! This is so true."

The metaphysical concepts it wove through the storyline validated many experiences I had as an intuitive and sensitive child. I realized that the imaginary world that consoled me through years of abuse had actually been filled with very real metaphysical experiences, magical beings and angelic support. The book opened the door to my awareness to previous experiences and gave me a sense of empowerment that had been missing from my life.

It was so refreshing. The fact that I was not alone in my search for greater meaning was validated when the New York Times ranked *The Celestine Prophecy* on the bestseller list. My quest to seek more was launched.

The 'good girl' in me and the beliefs I possessed about how to live a good life, were challenged next. I had a secure job with a good pension. I had a husband, the nice house with the picket fence and two kids. Yet, I wanted more. I started imagining my potential and seeing that so much more was available to me. I realized life could be richer than what I was experiencing.

I plunged diligently into metaphysical studies and soon found my courage increasing. I decided to apply to post-secondary school to improve my vocational skills and become a certified joint venture analyst. That critical voice in my head, left behind by my parents, began to fade. It did not take me long to land a great job in my new career.

As my career took off, my marriage ended. I moved into my own house with my children. I was working in a good job with a pension. This new lifestyle afforded me the ability to seriously explore more learning. I began the quest of understanding what life could be, based on new experiences and teachings. I became a '*seeker*'. I jokingly considered myself to be the '*queen of learning*', and still do.

Blessings in Disguise

After a few years of hard work, I scaled the tower of success. I had my own beautiful office in the corporate high rise, with a stunning view of the city. I was afforded my own corporate credit card, expense account and even ergonomically-designed furniture. I had made it! This elusive job with a good pension, that my early teachings had promised me, was now mine! Now I was out in front!

And then it happened.

One morning my life changed as I sat in my office with a letter from HR, letting me know I had been fired. In that moment, I felt fear and wondered how I was going to pay my mortgage. Then, with all my years of metaphysical studies, my fearful thoughts immediately shifted as I intuitively knew this was a gift from the Universe. I had been given the opportunity to lean on the metaphysical teachings I had been relentlessly studying. I realized I had to continue in my quest and start serving my soul's purpose in a bigger way. The release from this consuming J.O.B. would now provide me the time to do whatever I wanted.

The delivery of that letter transformed my life. I made the choice to take charge of my life and reinvent myself. Moving forward from that moment, I created my own business as a Master Intuitive Healer. I had hidden my gifts since I was a child, as I had been told they were the work of the devil. I now see the world through spiritual eyes and I'm able to feed my soul while also making a significant difference in the world. I now intuitively advise other *seekers* how to explore their own untapped higher wisdom.

My message to women is to remind them to awaken to their imagination and bring forth that little girl that once dreamed big dreams. The journey from religion to spirituality is a journey many women are taking. If you are a woman leading someone else's life rather than your own, just know there is something more for you. You are not your past, and you are not here to settle for second best.

Sometimes when things happen in your life, you may have difficulty seeing the situation as a blessing in disguise. In hindsight, every event in your life is divinely occurring to help you open up to those parts of you that have been shut down. Trust that there is a greater Source caring for you and live your life by following your heart, rather than your ego.

Lastly, connect with a community of like-minded women who only want to support and empower you to succeed. This is one of the greatest gifts we as women can give ourselves. I am so grateful for all the women, who have become my wonderful friends and have shown me how to create my own life by design, rather than by default.

I now know who I am and I LOVE my life. I am at peace with myself.

About Paige

Paige Stevensen is a positive and engaging intuitive healer. She didn't know that the abilities she had as a child – to see, hear, feel, and know the things that she did – weren't common to everyone.

Paige learned to trust her intuition to guide her through traumatic childhood experiences, a love-less marriage, two near-death experiences, and job layoffs.

Paige lives in beautiful British Columbia with her sweetie and her four-legged fur-family feline named Ebony, who, not surprisingly, is also intuitive.

In September 2017 she is releasing her much awaited program called "The Illuminated Practitioner Program (T.I.P.P.)"

You can connect with Paige at www.theintuitiveadvisor.com

I AM a brilliant woman because like an architect I have created my own masterpiece, and am now living the dream!!

~ Paige Stevensen

I AM Truth

Honour My Truth

By Dana Harrison

Something Lost…Something Gained.

Can you imagine being a woman who is 5'3" tall and 280 pounds? Well, that was me seven years ago. This is what my childhood, littered with sexual abuse, emotional trauma, teenage years filled with self-doubt and angst, an adult life complete with broken relationships and unfulfilled wanderlust ended up looking like for me. On that day, seven years ago, I looked in the mirror and didn't recognize the reflection staring back at me. Sure, I recognized the physical being; the blonde hair, sparkly blue eyes and the non-stop smile that masked the sadness and pain. I saw for the first time, my forgotten soul. My soul stared back at me and helped me to acknowledge the armour that had protected me from the past hurts, failures and wounds that I had been carrying around for almost 35 years. I knew my truth was hiding in there somewhere, protected by layers of self-loathing.

With pain and trauma present in many different ways, some turn to substance abuse as a way to numb and contain the past hurts. Frustrated children may act out and eventually become angry, destructive adults. Thankfully, I chose another path. I was a perfectionist, a constant high achiever who people looked up to. I was the "Go To" person who could always "fix" problems. Yet, the one thing I couldn't fix was my weight. As I reflected on who I had become and the truth of me being 280 lbs., I suddenly realized that I was morbidly obese. How did this happen?

I seriously suffered from "Shallow Hal" Syndrome. I was Gwyneth Paltrow. I had never seen myself the way I really was. On the outside, I was a confident, fun loving, amazing woman who seemed to have it all together. I spent years on and off diets, always losing and gaining the same 50 pounds, and developed coping mechanisms to ensure that I didn't have to face the demons within. I maintained huge walls around my soul, only opening windows now and again to let people see a glimpse of the real me.

"Fat people" (and let's face it…no one likes that word, but we all say or think it) tend to take two different paths; we are either the life of the party, the funny one who owns the room and is the center of attention or we choose to remain in the shadows. Either way, the outcome remains the same. Very few people know us really well because we hide behind our layers. In that moment, I declared there would be no more hiding from MY TRUTH. I saw a glimpse of the powerful, inspiring and brilliant woman that I knew I was capable of being. It was time to stop wearing my pain for all to see. I knew in that moment my life would never be the same.

Like everything else in my life, I approached my new journey head on, full steam ahead. I needed to lose the weight of an ***entire person*** to be healthy. WOW…when I put it that way, it seemed insurmountable. I had another secret I was keeping, that had contributed to my weight gain. Confronting it would set me free and release me from being a prisoner in my mind, body and soul. That journey began after spending hours researching The Good, The Bad and The Ugly about Gastric Bypass Surgery.

I found so many inspiring stories online of women whose backgrounds were the same as mine. Sadly, I did not have to look far to find the statistics of the link between Sexual Abuse and Obesity. Of the patients going through the process to have Bariatric Surgery, 40-75% have disclosed being sexually abused as children. In Canada, 1 in 3 women are sexually assaulted in their lifetime and a very high percentage of those women build the same walls and layers around them that I did. I no longer felt alone with my secret and took great comfort in knowing that others had overcome similar struggles. Article titles ranged from "Wearing Your Weight as Armour" to "Toxic Stress From Childhood Trauma Causes Obesity". It became my mission to become one of the success stories.

My Journey was set to begin. Thankfully in Ontario, Weight Loss Surgery (WLS) is covered by the Provincial Health Plan. After a load of tests and the comment, "Well you are the healthiest Fat Person I know", my family physician referred me for Bariatric Surgery in November 2009. With this part of the Journey came a whole new set of stressors. Would I be 'good enough' to be approved for the surgery? I told very few people what I was doing. Telling people would also be admitting that I had let my demons win. I didn't want to face the fact that I had failed at something.

I felt so alone and isolated at a time when I needed so much support. The thought of being turned down for the surgery consumed me. As part of the program, I needed to be approved by a nurse, dietician, social worker, psychologist and a surgeon. I also knew that it could take over a year to go through the mandatory program and be approved for surgery. As luck would have it, I got called for the first information session just 2 months after my referral went in. By the time I saw the dietician 2 months later, I had lost 25 pounds. Would I still be approved for the surgery? Would losing weight make them think I could do it on my own?

During my appointment, the dietician addressed my fears. Of the morbidly obese patients who lose more than fifty pounds, 80% will not keep it off. It becomes the vicious cycle that I had already been living for years. The dietician was concerned that I had set a weight goal that she deemed to be unrealistic and NEVER attainable. I wanted to weigh 127 pounds, which was half of the weight I was that day and the mid-point in having a "Normal BMI". After being obese for over fifteen years, statistics showed that the odds were not with me. Next up was the nurse's appointment. She echoed the dietician's opinion and stated I would never make my goal - but she also approved me for the surgery.

The next appointments were with the social worker and psychologist; they were the 'make or break' appointments. I had already undergone over a year of weekly in-depth counselling at the local Sexual Assault Centre and had seen many mental health professionals over the years, but never before was so much riding on my 'story'. I was ready to 'Honour My Truth' and make it work in my favour. Both appointments were scheduled for the same day and I took the day off from work. I was prepared for the feelings that I knew those appointments would resurface. At both appointments, I was open and honest about not having very much support. Like other things I had done solo in my life, this would be no different. We explored how I had ended up morbidly obese and about the work I had already done with professionals.

Both the social worker and psychologist voiced concerns about my goals and how much weight I wanted to lose. They had been warned about my 'unrealistic goals' by both the Nurse and the Dietician. I explained that I managed to accomplish all the other goals I had set in my life and knew that this would be no different. I walked out of those appointments feeling lighter than I had ever felt in my life. Honouring my TRUTH had set me free!

I was given a surgery date in September of the same year. Out of the blue, I got a phone call in mid-April asking if I wanted to have surgery in seven short days. The stars had lined up in the universe and my journey had just hit fast forward. The night prior to surgery, through tears, I updated my Will and Power of Attorney. Everything became VERY real that night and the realization set in that I was changing my life and nothing would ever be the same.

The ride to the hospital the next morning was very quiet, as I contemplated how I got to this place. I walked into the hospital alone, but it felt right. No one else could do the work that needed to be done. I was solely responsible for everything that was to come next. On that day, I weighed 245 pounds. Surgery went off without a hitch and the following months were filled with learning about my newly re-routed digestive system, while watching myself literally wither away in front of my eyes. I finally felt like I was morphing into what I always thought I was.

With every pound that I lost, I felt lighter and more free, both physically and spiritually. By my six month follow up, I had lost a total of 140 pounds from my start weight of 280, and 105 pounds since my surgery date. I was NORMAL BMI!!!!!! The clinic staff were amazed at my progress. I was determined to get to the goal weight I had set for myself - the same one that every health professional said I would NEVER get to. Seven and a half months after surgery, I weighed in at 127 pounds. I had done it. I was so proud of myself!

Now the hard work began. The first eighteen months after weight loss surgery is called the 'Honeymoon Period'. This is when it is very easy to lose weight. Those around you build you up because you are losing weight and looking great. There is a spring in your step that screams, "I've Got This" and you feel like you can conquer the world. Most weight loss surgery patients achieve their goal weight within the first eighteen months. After that, a feeling of "Now What?" sets in. For so many months, my life was consumed with weighing, measuring and tracking my food as I watched the scale go down and down and down. Once I hit my goal, I felt almost lost. This is the time when so many people start to regain the weight. The joke in the Weight Loss Surgery community is, "I hit goal weight…for 5 minutes". That was not going to be me. I would not go back to the dark place I had been. There had to be more. I knew that I was meant to DO more.

This Journey is so incredibly emotional and very little time or resources are provided around the 'Why'. Obesity, for most, is a physical manifestation of deeper issues. Unless you have 'been there, done that', it is often very hard to understand or provide support. Many people had a hard time understanding how I could be obese for so many years, yet I managed to maintain a healthy weight after the surgery. Questions like, "Why were you fat in the first place?" and "Do you think surgery was the easy way out?" were asked of me on a regular basis. I didn't often share the real reasons for why I had gained weight. Instead, I hid my secret and said things like, "Life got in the way" to deflect from the truth.

That all changed one night when I was out for dinner with a group of women, most of whom did not know my story. It came time to order dinner and the questions started from both the server and the women I was dining with. "Are you gluten intolerant?" "Is that an allergy or a preference?" I was very open and honest about my weight loss surgery and how I needed to eat, in order to maintain my results. Then a woman point blank asked me, "Why were you fat in the first place?" I put down my fork and pondered for a moment. There was no turning back. This would be the first time outside of support groups and my close family and friends, that I would speak about the 'How and Why' of my journey. "I was sexually and emotionally abused for most of my childhood and I chose to wrap myself in many layers to protect me," were the words I chose to answer with.

The woman who had asked the question actually spit out her drink in shock. The others who were within earshot averted their eyes and were not sure what to say. As I sat a little taller, the woman who had asked the question that many think, but few have the courage to ask, quickly tried to compose herself and answered back with, "I am so sorry". I reassured her that there was nothing to be sorry for. Our past makes us who we are and I was ready to embrace all of it and make it work for me instead of against me. I was ready to speak my truth. Another woman at the table thanked me for sharing and asked if it was ok if she asked questions. We ended up sharing stories of our pasts and the effect they have on us every day for hours. In that moment, I knew that I was meant to share my story with others, both within and outside of the Weight Loss Surgery community. It became my mission to help people find their courage and their voice, just as I had done. Out of that evening came an appearance on a radio program and an opportunity to share my story of 'Trauma to Triumph' with others.

I had exposed my soul as I had never done before, and there was great freedom in that. My gift in sharing my story is to remind women to stop being afraid of revealing what they have hidden away for years, as sometimes that is the key to growth. Sharing my story would let others know that they are not alone and that change was possible. I had moved to a place of acceptance and was confident that my past would never consume or define me again. As all of the pieces came together, there was a clear vision of what was yet to come.

For so many years, I had lived in the shadows of shame with a broken soul. Now, I no longer needed protection from the pain and hurts of my past. I finally had the confidence and desire to channel them and rise up, using their energies to propel me onward and upward, instead of inward to that very dark place I had been locked in for so many years.

When others challenge you with, "You can't do that" or "Are you sure that is realistic?", know that you have the strength within you to conquer anything you commit to doing. With great goals and great work come great rewards. You possess the courage and passion to embrace healing instead of pain, and only when you do that will you be able to 'Honour Your Truth'!

About Dana

Dana Harrison is an Author and Speaker who relocated from Ontario to Calgary, Canada two years ago. She is the Co-Leader of a Bariatric Surgery Support Group in Alberta and remains very active in many Weight Loss Surgery Support Groups in Canada.

Dana believes that we all have the potential to live up to our greatest potential by honouring our truth and harnessing its power to work for you instead of against you. By sharing her stories of Trauma to Triumph, Dana has enlightened, empowered and inspired others by speaking across Canada in person and on the radio.

Dana lives in Calgary with her daughter Zoe and their cats. She spends quality time with her older daughter, Alexis, in B.C. Dana is passionate about travel, great food, interior design and loves the colour pink.

You can connect with Dana at honouryourtruth.com

I am a brilliant woman because I Honour My Truth by sharing my story to inspire others.

~ Dana Harrison

I AM Nurturing

Second Adulthood

By Donna Malchuk

"I don't love you anymore." The declaration made by my husband sent a shock wave through my body, putting me into fight mode. My fists found his chest as I pounded my anger into him. The pounding then moved to the wall as my body slid into a puddle on the floor. Life as I knew it had ended and a new transformation had begun. Little did I know that this stage was a natural rite of passage for humanity. Mine started with the ending of a twenty-six year partnership and has transformed into a new relationship with 'Self'.

I grew up in an alcoholic family that was filled with emotional drama. This created an addiction to adrenalin in me. Unknowingly, this set me up to continuously look for the next 'drama' or to create one. That was my life, both as a child and as an adult. It gets tiresome at some point for the people around you - even for the ones that love you. That is exactly the point my husband had hit. My grown kids were off to university and he was done. There was no amount of reconciliation that I could negotiate. You cannot make someone love you or make someone work on a relationship to make it better. You simply cannot make someone stay if they want to go. The busyness of family life had ended and had thrown me into my Self.

We each have our own journey to process and going out on my own opened a space for a new magnificence to unfold. The mid-point of life was forced upon me and as I looked in the mirror, I did not recognize the person looking back at me. Despite having done personal psychological healing and spiritual work, I realized I was not exempt from this inevitable stage in life.

I developed a new addiction, and replaced my need for drama for one of experiencing peace and harmony. I found that the busy-making ended when I could now just be responsible for myself. 'Doing' was replaced with 'Being'. I no longer cared to strive for the 'Canadian Dream'. I began to pare down for a simpler life, which made room for what was yet to come.

Change is never easy, especially when your life's dreams have been shattered. I knew that denying the process of change and grief would create a crisis, so I utilized my sources of support to go through all the emotions of loss and grief. While sorting out the divorce, I had already experienced the stages of denial, anger and bargaining. I now dove into the stage of melancholy and allowed myself time to process; time to heal.

At some point, I came out of the depths of despair. My days became sunnier as I realized that I could fill them however I desired. I was now the creator of my own life, without any responsibility to others. This was an amazing realization. Each day, I would wake up and decide how the day would be spent. I got to create my life just as I wanted. I found excitement in each day, and my life became filled with peace and happiness. Little did I know that there was more to this story and I was just at the edge of a new mountain.

The first trigger came when I entered a new relationship and he eventually moved into my home. Combining the material elements of two homes was a challenge. I had to give up more of my stuff and bring in things I did not necessarily desire. I chose to compromise and overlook things. Then, I had to change my daily routine to accommodate the needs of my new partner. I adjusted. Gradually, I found that I was slipping back into my old habit of placing another person's needs ahead of my own. I felt like I was losing touch with my *self* and with what was important to ME. My time for self-reflection was replaced with unconscious TV watching with my beloved. The time I used to spend on profound inspirational writing became interrupted by his call for attention. It irritated me and caused me to feel resentful. Gradually, I became tired, lethargic and even lost my desire to live. What's it all about anyway? I didn't want my old life back. I wanted my new life, the simpler life that I had had a taste of. Conflict permeated my mind. How could I stay in a relationship, but still hold on to the new life that I had created and had come to enjoy?

The next trigger came from going through menopause. Hot flashes, weight gain, memory loss and frequently being irritated, resulted in me starting to feel much older than I was. My life had filled up with negativity and low vibrational 'being'. Everyday seemed to be a repeat of the one before, with nothing new or exciting. I was just going through the motions. Things that used to make me happy, no longer did. I entered into a cycle of judgment, complaining and becoming bitter instead of striving to become better. I didn't want any part of this kind of life. Getting old scared me. Thoughts of dying and what that all meant, filled my mind. I was facing my own mortality head-on. I arrived at the next stage of life…

Midlife transition is new to our society. During the 1500s to 1850, life expectancy was just 40 years. There was no reaching mid-life, as we know it today. By the 1900s, life expectancy had gradually risen to 47 years. It is just in the last century that a dramatic rise in life expectancy took place. Today, life expectancy has risen to 83 years and has created an opportunity for a relatively new rite of passage to occur called, 'the Mid-Life Transition'. No one is exempt, no matter how organized or spiritual we are. At some point, we all face our own mortality. When we do, we will be called to either rise above our fears and transform how we live our lives - or succumb to our fears and fall into crisis. Today, we are blessed with better health and longer lives. This blessing comes with new challenges. A new awareness and understanding will be required to successfully navigate this amazing opportunity.

As I researched 'Mid Life Transition', I learned that it is just as important a stage as the transition from childhood to puberty. I also learned that since it is so new to humanity, we are not yet talking about it. We do not understand it. Most people do not even consider it an issue, even when they are going through it themselves.

Some people feel trapped or tied down by the responsibilities of the ones that love them and they run away from this opportunity to grow. They may try to return to the place in their past where they experienced their most joy and a life of energy – their teenage years! They buy a fast car, attend parties and are attracted to the stimulating youthfulness of hot younger people. Others may lose their interest in life and just give up all together, not realizing they still have another thirty years to live. Either way, life as they knew it, was over!

That was where I had fallen, I had given up. I did not understand that this phase was a call to the next phase of my own life. I didn't yet know that I could process it and create a new and deeper life experience. All I knew was that I was sick and tired of being sick and tired. I needed a new perspective.

In the Western world, and the first half of our lives, we are groomed by society to focus our energy on achieving goals: getting an education, a good job and creating a family. Once we have that in place, we start to wonder what we will do for the second half of our lives. Some go back and start over again. Some stay stuck in life as they know it. Some yearn for something more, but don't know exactly what that is or how to get it. What 'that' is, is the next stage of humanity – second adulthood. How we enter it, is by processing the transition from living a goal-oriented lifestyle to living a BEING-oriented lifestyle. This next stage is calling us to reset our life to better reflect our heart and soul's desire. We get to transform life as we know it, to a deeper meaning and experience. We move from a past of 'doing', to a future of 'being' as we create a Soul-lived life.

With my newfound knowledge, I knew that there was a major mind, body and soul transformation about to take place. The perfect place to begin was with my mind. I had to get out of my head. I have a very strong mind and it wants to think, think, think. I can think myself into very dark holes. After my second child was born, I had a major stress reaction to the great responsibility of caring for two small children. I expressed it by pounding and kicking on my walls. That was the first time my husband had to intervene and find me some help. The psychiatrist diagnosed me as having a strong case of, "Stinking Thinking". He taught me how to pause and get into a state of mindlessness to find a moment's peace. My mind is so strong, that it is an entity unto itself and it takes all my will power to keep it from running away with ME. It is a constant exercise, even after thirty years of practice. I still have to re-mind my SELF that this is my addictive dis-ease and challenge, requiring continuous persistence and present moment awareness.

Next to come was *bodywork*. My daughter returned home to spend a few weeks between university graduation and her new job abroad. I was complaining to her that I had so many aches and pains and that every day was a struggle for me to just get out of bed in the morning. She stated that she was concerned for me as well, as I had put on a lot of weight. She also didn't like that we sat around every evening, watching TV. One day we were shopping in our neighbourhood mall and noticed a new vendor. As we went over to check it out, we noticed that it was a new gym. I was strongly encouraged by my daughter to sign up. It turned out to be a great decision. I had to book classes and stick to them, or the gym charged extra for missing. After a few months, I felt my energy increasing and the aches and pains subsiding. Just getting out and moving my body made all the difference. Now when I miss a few weeks due to being on a vacation, my body reminds me what I am missing and I can't wait to get back to the gym. Movement, at this stage of my life, is very important for my body, as well as my mind.

Despite being more effective at looking after my body and my thoughts, there was still a sadness permeating my being. I just couldn't seem to shake it and find my happiness quotient like I used to. My soul still felt sad. Through the internet, a new healer came to me. After a discussion with her, she said that I was experiencing, 'soul lose'. She initiated a guided visualization with me and then did a ritual healing to 'call in my Soul'. Immediately after the session, I felt a sense of childlike energy permeating my body. My smile returned and I felt like dancing. Happiness swept over me again. It was interesting to learn of 'soul lose' and I wanted to know more.

My research on 'soul lose' lead to the Mayan healing arts. I learned that they believe in four situations that can cause 'spiritual illness' or soul loss. These situations are usually brought on by trauma or shock. I was apparently suffering from "Tristeza" – Sadness, and "Pesar" – Grief, which was not totally expressed and cleared from my divorce. The other two spiritual illnesses related to bullying or jealousy. They were called "Invidia" – Envy and "Susto" – Fright.

The Mayan treatments for the various spiritual illnesses are all very similar. A bath regime using specific herbs was recommended to heal my Spiritual dis-ease. The awareness of the reality of soul loss and soul retrieval was an epiphany for me. I can now see this dis-ease in people around me, especially in elders. I've come to understand that successfully moving through a mid-life transition may also involve reconnecting to our soul.

I have now embraced this next stage of life, "second adulthood". I understand that it is a process of transformation and that I can pause in awareness, while I wait for what is next to come. I can examine the possibilities and consider new options with wonder and excitement. I see it as an opportunity to change my routine and how I move in the world. I now give my Self space to grow into something new, as I deepen my experience in this new chapter of my life. Life isn't over, YET! I am now choosing to engage and live life to the fullest. WooHoo!

About Donna

Donna Malchuk has been on a lifetime search for the meaning and why we are really here. Dealing with a childhood with an alcoholic parent, she healed the dis-ease of codependency, and was supported through the healthy and awakened parenting of her own two children. She found a sense of responsibility and created security and abundance, while coaching other women to seek wholeness through awakening their feminine radiance and reclaiming their true identity. She narrated this experience of her childhood and early adulthood in her book "A Path to Perfect Love: One Woman's Journey to Love after love Through Conscious Living".

Donna now seeks a more fulfilling and enriched awakened life experience in the remaining third of this human lifetime, through a deeper connection to truth and the practice of true spiritual realization, which is at the heart of being. Donna is not a solitary life traveler, therefore creates community of like-minded travelers, to collaborate and support those on a same enlightening journey. Donna lives, and practices coaching and other modalities, in Calgary, AB.

Connect with Donna at www.HeartOfBeing.ca

I am a brilliant woman, whom inspires and nurtures others to the heart of their Being.

~ Donna Malchuk

I AM Powerful

Soulfully Chosen

By Amy van Meijl

Sometimes, our greatest cause of suffering is our family. They are supposed to love us unconditionally, support us in all things and be a safe haven in a storm, but sometimes that is not the family we find ourselves with. As a result, when deep hurts and soul-piercing pain are delivered at the hands of our family members, we have to learn how to move through life on our own. I've had to learn how to protect myself from the words and actions of my family, and though I love each member dearly and unconditionally, I've learned the cost of doing so blindly.

I do not blame my family, for without the pain and suffering I experienced, I would not be who I am today. I trust that in sharing my story, I may help another soul to rise up out of their hurt and create a beautiful life.

Growing up was tough for me. I always felt out of place with my family; I often fought with my sister and grew up feeling unheard, unconnected and with the belief driven into me that I was the cause of the strife within our home. I learned to be independent very early and that it was up to me to take care of myself.

I remember when I was maybe ten or eleven, we had gone into the city for a family weekend. My family and I were walking in the park one morning; I must have been misbehaving because I remember my dad kicking me, and not in a playful way. As I scooted to get away, I instinctively put my hand behind me to protect myself and as the kick landed, pain exploded into my hand. At breakfast, I couldn't move my hand. It hurt so much, but I was dismissed by everyone. A few days later, my mom finally took me to the doctor. After a set of x-rays, the doctor stated that my hand had actually been broken.

I am the second of four kids and my older sister and I seemed to always butt heads. She would tease me mercilessly. When I would react, she'd go after me harder. It became even worse after my parents separated. One week after my 14th birthday, we moved from our home on the farm to a two-bedroom apartment. It was crowded with my mom, my two sisters, my brother, our two pets and I. Life was no picnic before and now it only got worse.

As we grew older, my older sister continued after me without fail. My sister developed a much bigger chest than I and she constantly teased me and pointed out hurtfully that I had such small boobs. I tried everything I could think of to make it stop and when I couldn't bear it any longer, I finally decided to ask Mom for help.

I'll never forget that night. My mom and I weren't close; years of having to figure things out on my own had ensured that. Filled with shame and fear, I went to my mom one night before bed. I tried to calmly tell her how much it hurt me that my sister teased me about my small chest. I told her of how I had been on the phone with my boyfriend and my sister declared loudly so he could hear, that she 'didn't understand why he would even date me, I had NO boobs'. I told mom that I had tried everything to make it stop but that I had run out of ideas. At 15, feeling completely exposed, I'll never forget my mom….. laughing at me. She said sisters tease and that I was just being oversensitive. I knew then that I would never find an ally in my mom when it came to my sister.

I eventually created what felt like a great life. I had earned my bachelor's degree in environmental design, I had a job, my own apartment, tons of friends and a sexy boyfriend. Then, at the age of 28 my life completely unraveled. I was let go from my job six days into the new year and the guy I was head over heels for dumped me out of the blue. I was facing the reality of failure and moving back into my mom's house, which meant I was moving away from the life I had been building for years - my friends, my gym, my church - everything that brought me joy, a sense of purpose and who I was. I felt hollow, empty. I'd lay awake at night, staring at the stars, begging God to show me why this had happened. I truly thought nothing else could possibly go wrong, but six weeks after moving back to mom's, I was told to leave. I was no longer welcome. In my darkest hour, my family, who had said they would 'always' be there for me, deserted me.

All the fears and doubts I had felt my whole life were suddenly confirmed. I knew then I was entirely alone. My life had turned to dust and, though I had been told my family would always support me, when I needed their love and understanding most, they turned away from me. I had felt lost in my life before, and I have felt lost since, but I have never felt as utterly adrift as I did in those months.

I stumbled through the next several months blindly, firmly believing I was to learn something from this, but not having any idea what that was to be. My dearest friend became my lifeline. She helped me move out of my mom's house, unpacked all my boxes and made sure I was eating. She checked in with me constantly and, gradually, as the wounds began to fade and the pain was no longer quite so acute, I began to come alive again.

In the autumn, I traveled to the Netherlands for my older sister's wedding. In conversations with my extended family, I was surprised to find empathy for me over the actions of my immediate family. Experiencing that solidarity in my pain finally allowed me to find the strength within to move forward. Three weeks later, upon returning to Canada, I began rebuilding my life.

I started a new job back in the city I'd left and reconnected with my friends, my gym and my church. I moved into a better apartment than I'd had before. I was blessed by a boss who saw ability in me and, through his encouragement, I began to look for ways I could grow professionally. Eighteen months later, I followed my heart and moved to Calgary to be with my amazing partner, Dave. It was the first decision I'd ever made that I knew was absolutely right for me, down to my core. I then made the second such decision when I decided to start my own interior design business. It was a dream I had had for years. Despite massive fear and trepidation, I was rooted in an absolute knowing that it was going to be a success. My deepest instinct, my soul, vibrated 'Yes!'

For two years, I worked diligently at my business, learning and growing both the business and myself. I experienced some success and had wonderful clients. Then, last summer I was dealt another blow by my family that brought me to my knees.

My mom had been out to Alberta a few weeks before to visit me, but the visit had ended with a negative conversation. Now, my mom was in the hospital and I had gone back to Manitoba to help my siblings take care of her. When I arrived, I couldn't understand why all of my family seemed so distant to me. Dave had stayed in Alberta as we were renovating our house, so I was alone. Five days after I had arrived, at 5AM one morning, I rushed to the hospital to be with my mom as she couldn't breathe. I was trying to keep her calm while we waited for the doctor by showing her videos of my niece on her phone, when I read it: A group chat I had been excluded from, yet it was all about me. It seemed that negative conversation had been twisted against me and sold as truth, unquestioningly, to my siblings.

Afterward, I was reeling. I couldn't find my footing. I no longer knew who I could trust and my faith in myself was shaken like someone had torpedoed my soul. My relationships with my mom and siblings were shattered and my heart became fragmented. I tried to move past it, tried to release the hurt and confusion, all the while protecting myself from further hurt by distancing myself from my family. I tried to focus on all the good that was happening in my world, my amazing partner, my dear friends and my fabulous clients, all whilst I was unknowingly sinking into a deep depression.

It hit me between the eyes when Dave came home from an evening out. I had been sitting at home desperately lonely and afraid, and he told me that a noted politician had died in a plane crash. 'He is so lucky', was my very first thought. Seconds later, the weight of that hit me and I knew something needed to change.

That night, I couldn't sleep. I was so deeply lost in a dark hole, but I'd had to keep up my happy, positive face for everyone around me. I got out of bed and sobbed. I sobbed for who I had become, for the 'me' I had pushed away, for the pain I couldn't show to the rest of the world. As my body heaved from the weight and the hurt I had been burying for so long, I knew I needed to reach out and my soul whispered, 'Message Karen.' I knew of and admired Karen (*creator of this book series*) as a successful woman, though I hadn't really had much of a relationship with her. Moving entirely on faith, I reached out.

I said 'yes' to her guiding me on how to put the pieces of my soul back together again. I felt so small the first time we met, fearing that I'd have to keep up the ruse that, I was doing great! I felt like a lost child and as I told the story of what happened, the hurt and pain came pounding forward again. Session after session, I learned how to reveal the deep hurts, beliefs and patterns that I had ingrained in myself, and I began to realize, I had been forcing myself to live small. I always felt that I had a bigger purpose in this world, but fear, uncertainty and the desire to be loved had kept me squishing myself into an ever-shrinking box.

I began to see that my family was soulfully chosen by me, and that, while their actions were deeply hurtful, they were not bad people. Their actions were expressions of the deep hurts they had all endured, wounds that had been buried and not yet healed and I realized that only unhealed people hurt other people.

As I continued my sessions, I recognized that I truly do have a massive purpose for good in this world and that all the hurt and pain I had experienced at the hands of my family was actually their soul's way of pushing me out of the nest so that I would stretch out my wings and fly! I now had a choice: I could choose to use those experiences as an excuse, and continue to live a life filled with guilt and manipulation, OR I could choose to rise above and BE the person I'd always dreamed of. I could become the powerhouse of change I envisioned and let my own healed soul help others.

In my interior design business, my biggest driving purpose is always to help my clients create a home that is truly about them, a home that supports them wholly and fully. I never knew why that was so integral in me until I started to put the lessons and experiences together in my life. All I ever wanted was to be loved for who I truly am and to be positively supported, to live the life I dreamed of. In my relationship with Dave, the two things I strive for above everything else is to make sure he knows how deeply and fully he is loved and to have continual, open and honest communication so that we can create the life we dream of together. That has now become the cornerstone for the massive work I feel I am preparing for in this world. To help others create spaces that truly reflect who they are, to help them know they are deeply and unequivocally loved and to help create open lines of communication through their homes, in their relationships and in the world.

Through all this, I've learned these key lessons:

1. **Always trust your intuition, your inner vibration.** When you energetically vibrate 'Yes!' to an opportunity or decision ~ trust it. It is your soul speaking to you. If you

feel the red flag of a 'No', trust that your soul is watching out for you.

2. **We become who we choose to be**. Using your past as an excuse is just you lying to yourself. You are who and how you are today because you chose to be. You can see your past pains and experiences as concrete boots holding you down, or you can use those experiences as jet fuel to become who you want to be.
3. **Dream big and LIVE BIG!** If you are holding yourself down hoping to earn love, respect or acceptance, you are robbing yourself of your dreams and robbing the world of the true soul that lives inside you. You might be dreaming big, but you are living small. Dream big and LIVE BIG!

I am still learning the way and I do not know exactly where my massive purpose will take me, but I know this: If I continue to live small, I not only deny my soul's yearning, I also deny the world of the massive positive change that I am to bring about. From here on in, I am consciously choosing who I will be, trusting my inner vibration as I move into uncharted waters and I am bursting out of my self-imposed box to live big! In faith, I am stepping into the amazing love and true honesty of who I am, trusting that the universe will not let me fail, but will stretch my wings so that I can fly.

For Lois, who always believed in me.

About Amy

Originally a farm girl from western Manitoba, Amy followed her heart and moved to Calgary, Alberta to be with her love and amazing partner, Dave. Soon after, she began Dutch Touch Interiors, launching a dream she'd held for nearly a decade. Her humble beginnings gave her down-to-earth roots and, leading heart-first, she assists her clients to determine the needs of their home, drawing out each personality while guiding them to create a home they deeply love. Through her warmth and approachable manner, Amy connects with even the most unsure client to claim their true inner style and feel confident in their design decisions.

In 2016, after only 2 years in business, Dutch Touch Interiors was listed among the Top 30 Interior Design Companies in Calgary by Point 2 Homes.

Connect with Amy at www.dutchtouchinteriors.com.

I am a brilliant woman as I trust my inner vibration and choose to be a powerful force of positive change!

~ Amy van Meijl

I AM Resilient

Following My Messy Bliss

Surviving early motherhood with some bumps, twists and turns; a dash of style, grace, creativity; and a sprinkling of fairy dust.

By Sandra Catania

I recently saw a meme on social media, which read, *"If you are going to be a mess, you may as well be a hot mess."* I giggled and deeply identified with this statement. More and more as I get older, I'm learning to accept, respect, admire, and treasure all the "quirks" that make me who I am.

Since becoming a mother nine years ago, my life has been quite the rollercoaster ride of self-discovery. This journey is full of peaks and valleys, an experience that has truly been body, mind, soul, spirit and heart expanding, with many lessons learned. I'm going to take you through the highlights, and the lows too. I trust, I will impart some insights that I have gained along the way to others embarking on this path.

It all began with forgiveness, which was my first step towards healing - forgiving myself for my imperfections, shortcomings, and what I saw as failures. Becoming responsible for two beautiful little beings completely overwhelmed me. We are so very hard on ourselves, aren't we? I have forgiven myself now, and have created my soft place to land, surrounded by people who love and support me, including myself.

It haunts me still, that last box of paperwork that was on my "to-do" list before my first baby came. Always the procrastinator (a quality I have since forgiven and embraced), I left this one, medium-sized box unfinished, unsorted and unorganized. It never did get sorted. And in the nine years and second baby that followed, that one box multiplied into a couple of dozen boxes. Yikes! Boxes upon boxes of my life since becoming a mom, all piled up in the basement. My passions and interests, all the tools and books and supplies that came with them, packed away, sitting around in disorganized, neglected piles.

What a powerful metaphor for what I had done to my life—putting everyone else's needs and wants before my own. This forced me to take all the vibrant, luminescent, sparkly, lively pieces of my personality and hide them away, stacked on top of each other, never to see the light of day. This is the reality I had created.

I struggled through many dark days, just trying to survive somehow, while desperately striving to keep everyone fed and clothed in a somewhat healthy and clean manner as I shuttled them to school and various activities. I completely lost touch with my body or any appreciation or interest in keeping it healthy and nourished; I lived in stained yoga pants and ponytails. I felt like a robot, going through the motions but not really being present or engaged in what I was doing. Joyless and so completely worn out from my duties as a mom, I felt lost and adrift most days. I was extremely unhappy, alone, isolated, and unappreciated nearly all of the time. Trapped in a downward spiral of negative thoughts and behaviours that I was not proud of, I felt like I had no control. The dark clouds of my mid-twenties (the second of three depressive episodes in my life) had sadly returned.

I have recently confronted and dealt with the sad fact that I experienced postpartum anxiety, on top of postpartum depression in early motherhood. This went undiagnosed and untreated for years. It is a topic which needs to be addressed, openly discussed, and solutions need to be found. The support that a new mom receives in our society is sorely lacking, and countless mothers around me experience these conditions. There's endless suffering and anguish that could be aided and even completely avoided by the addition of a more solid support system for those first early years when the risk is so high.

One thing I did well was to set up a postpartum doula for myself for those tender first few weeks, the exact time that *I* needed to be mothered. This may have been the smartest thing I ever did as a new mom. The nurturing I received from this incredible woman was both deeply needed and enormously appreciated. She took care of *ME*—made me lunch, changed the sheets on my bed, and taught me how to bathe my sweet, tiny angel baby safely. She always answered my thousands of questions about babies so patiently, without making me feel like a total clueless newbie. She told me to stay in my pyjamas and to keep sleeping until I felt I had enough rest. This was exactly what I needed. The support and guidance given to me by both my birth doulas and my postpartum doula were the most magical experiences of motherhood for me. Another shining example of sisterhood!

It was the months and years after that newborn period that I slowly but surely slipped deeper and deeper into despair from the lack of a proper network of professionals and friends to guide me through. The years of sleep deprivation, caused by my second baby (a horrible sleeper), turned me into a cranky, irritable 'mombie,' unable to cope or stay calm and patient on most days. I resorted to mom guilt and feelings of failure and self-loathing.

What is also sad and unfortunate is that my husband was battling issues of his own during this same time. He was emotionally unavailable to me for much of that time, which made it that much more difficult and lonely in my world. Thankfully, this has since been wholly accepted and forgiven as part of our journey.

Now, on the edge of the other side of this experience, I am happy to report that I have survived. I have thrived. I have taken on new adventures and passions. My life is heading in directions I am giddily excited about. I am proud of myself for how far I have come and continue to go, and the new risks and opportunities I am embracing almost daily. *"Always do things you are a little scared of,"* is a consistent life motto. It does absolutely and unequivocally pay off, every time.

What changes did I make to turn my life around? First, I found a therapist to help me talk it through. I began to realize the importance of self-care. The necessity (not luxury) of looking after *MY* own needs became extremely apparent. I asked for help from friends and relatives so that I could have some time away from my children. I let go of the guilt. Yes, *ALL* of it, because it was sabotaging any amount of pleasure or nurturing that I may have gained during that time I spent looking after myself.

I started to make sure I was filling my own cup on a consistent basis. I made time to do the things I love and feel passionate about, and took care of my physical body by swimming, doing yoga and other forms of exercise. I paid attention to what I was putting into my body, and added good quality water, supplements, and organic produce. I cleansed and detoxed when I felt my body had a need for it.

I took time to tend to my connection to Spirit by being in nature and attending my spiritual community services again on a more regular basis. I also returned to volunteering there. I followed my bliss whenever possible, which often led me to breathe in the beauty of Mother Nature, in the wild natural places close to me. I made trips to mountains and islands. I took time to ground myself in these places, and in my own home.

I made sure that I was dedicating efforts to socialize and connect with others by spending time with both friends and in women's circles. I embraced my gifts for connecting people by continuously building and expanding my network.

From a career perspective, I became interested and active in learning new skills. When the opportunity came along to expound upon my knowledge of reflexology, I took the course.

One of the most rewarding and empowering experiences came about very unexpectedly. My bliss showed up as a Facebook ad in my newsfeed from a local lingerie store called Bratopia. As part of their campaign about '#AuthenticBeauty,' they were sponsoring a modelling contest for four women, which included a trip to Las Vegas. The messages they were conveying impacted and inspired me. How refreshing to see an actual woman in these advertisements, instead of the 'unrealistic-to-98%-of-the-population' models who are usually featured. Whenever I saw their ads, I felt like cheering, *"Good for them! Good for her! Now THAT'S a cause I can get behind and support!"* We need to embrace every woman, in every shape and size. *We are all beautiful!* Suddenly I had that laser-sharp focused sensation and knew I was going to go to Vegas and be part of this movement. And so it happened.

Well, it wasn't really *that* easy. It took a truckload of courage to send that first email to let them know that I was interested in trying out. Palms sweaty, my chest tightening, butterflies dancing all around inside, I took a deep breath and clicked "send." Then my adventure began. As the day of the casting call approached, I became more and more nervous and seriously thought about calling the whole thing off several times. However, that little voice inside my head kept whispering and urging me to give it a try. *"What have I got to lose?"* the stronger voice reasoned with my scared, shrinking side. What *DID* I have to lose, really?

I talked myself into it and kept on making many preparations. Babysitter? *Check!* Hair? *Check!* Makeup? *Check!* Outfit? Almost there. It became more of a fun adventure rather than something I was dreading. I have always enjoyed dressing up and feeling pretty. But to have to present myself in just undergarments? That was indeed an entirely different story.

The upbeat energy and support on the panel of people interviewing us turned out to be the perfect atmosphere to just smile, be myself and adopt the, 'see what happens' attitude. I found out a week or so later that I had been chosen to be in the fashion show, news that both thrilled and terrified me. This was getting *REAL!*

I decided to use my nervous energy in a positive way and embarked on a detox and cleansing program, which gave me the clarity, focus, and energy I needed to bring my confidence up. My body has definitely not been the same since it grew and birthed two children into the world, but my belief is that it has gotten even more womanly and alluring with every stretch mark. I wear them with pride and embrace all my curves, including my breasts, which served me so well to nurse those babies into toddlerhood. This body is a miracle, a temple, an amazing instrument with which I walk through my days. It allows me to do so many incredible things, from swimming, to yoga, to making love. I am getting to know, love, and accept my body more and more as I age, and to appreciate everything it does and has done for me. My body is beautiful and worth celebrating.

Then there were the other Goddesses there. *WOW!* It was mind-blowing how gorgeous and unique each of them was. How quickly we all bonded and supported one another through one of the most nerve-wracking events of our lives, melted my heart. We were all there for the same reason, to say, *"Look at us, world! We are REAL and we are BEAUTIFUL, each in our own individual way. We are women, hear us ROAR!!!"*

Who knew there was so much fun to be had outside my comfort zone?

Fun was definitely the theme of the trip and the photoshoots. I've never laughed so much in my life. I think the fact that we were having the time of our lives is truly visible in the photos. I am so grateful to Bratopia for having this vision and making it come true, for helping women everywhere recognize and honour the Goddess who lives in each one of us.

Besides having experienced life as a supermodel for a week, what I came back to was the love and support of the sisterhood I have so carefully built. I've dug deep into tl [illegible] purpose of sharing my gifts of reflexology and my [illegible] oils with others, expressing my authentic self at [illegible] when it doesn't come easily. I have begun the proc[illegible] opening, sorting through, and examining all the various pieces of myself, in a kind and gentle manner. Just like those dusty boxes in the basement, the essence of *WHO I AM* is being unpacked, aired out, and getting to see the light of day. The light, which is contained in each one of us, is finally getting its chance to shine forth from me.

These are the elements that have gotten me through the toughest of times, and this is why I have to share my story. My past of being stuck in the illusions of not feeling good enough as a mom and not enjoying life did not serve me. My glorious triumph over deep, dark, overwhelming sadness now serves me, and those around me. It *CAN* be done, and it is definitely worth doing. I don't want others to suffer and struggle the way that I did. I want to share my shortcuts, tips, and tricks. My purpose has been found in helping others to feel better, to love themselves more, and to respect their own time and vision for their present and future happiness. We all deserve this.

About Sandra

Self described Goddess, Empress, Earth Angel and Hot Mess. Speaker of three languages, holder of two passports and an avid traveller, Sandra is happiest exploring new territory. She is a student of Reiki, yoga and homeopathy and a firm believer in the power of positive vibes. Sandra is mother to two marvellously rambunctious children, ages 5 and 9. She is also the creator of three networking groups for women, called "Calgary Goddess Groups".

Sandra is a sisterhood facilitator, reflexologist and independent oils consultant with Young Living Essential Oils. She believes strongly in magic, intuition, following her bliss and never giving up an opportunity for an adventure or great chocolate. She feels most in service to her community as a volunteer at her local Centre For Spiritual Living branch in Calgary, where she plans to eventually pursue her ministerial studies.

Connect with Sandra at www.goddessmommies.ca

I am a Brilliant woman because I rise again, each time brighter and stronger than the last.

~ Sandra Catania

I AM Passionate

The Courage to Speak . . . And Be Heard

By Elizabeth Bennett

I am a gay woman and proud of it! You would think that coming out of the closet to the world would be exciting news. It gets better!

Imagine this ~ a lesbian who is also a principal in a Catholic School. Go figure.

For years, I have witnessed students who are in the closet themselves, afraid to be whom they really are. It makes my heart sad. This is why I am writing my story. It has brought me to a place where I can no longer be silent about our children's struggles and their future. In this day and age, they should feel safe while living a full and productive, happy and joyful life. There needs to be a place for them to have the courage to be bold, and that allows them to be who they are, who they want to be, and to be proud of themselves for taking a stand for their lives. It all starts with being true to myself.

All these years I had been silent.

Home life as a child wasn't always the best of times. Frequently I listened to the sound of my father's voice yelling obscenities, berating and beating on my mother. Often I found myself huddled in my bed with the covers up around my ears and face, wishing for the dreadful noise to stop, worrying for my mother, and at times, wishing him dead.

My grandmother was my shelter and escape from reality. She knew what was occurring in my house, but she, like me, was helpless to do anything about it. As often as I could, I would spend time at her house, enjoying her company, wishing and praying that things would get better. It never did.

My mother would often speak to the priest at our church to ask for advice, only to be told that she should go home and work it out as it was her place to be with her man. I didn't quite understand how someone could go home to physical, emotional, spiritual, and financial abuse and continue to forgive, forget, and move on. Perhaps that's where my compassion came from in my growth as a young person into the strong, caring and powerful leader that I am today.

Although I had great relationships with guys, mostly playing football, dodgeball, street hockey or any type of game that brought us together in the community, it was an altogether different experience with girls. Wading through the masses at my high school, I experienced taunting and teasing, better known today as bullying. I learned quickly that I could not enter the girl's washroom for fear of being trapped, as I knew that was where the so-called 'cool girls' hung out. I was also aware of a small group of druggies, one of whom approached me and commented that she noticed I had great veins in my arms. She wondered if I would be interested in going with her to try something out with her friends. I gracefully and nervously declined, hoping that she wouldn't accost me outside of school. Not knowing what to do with all of this chaos in my life, at school and at home, I chose to find volunteer opportunities to escape from my own personal reality.

I didn't share my experiences with anyone ~ no one to talk to . . . who would understand anyway?

I discovered that I was surprisingly good at competitive bowling. It took me away from home and school. I felt an element of safety there. It was fun! I experienced peace and people even helped me to improve my skills. Bowling early on Saturday mornings was well worth looking forward to, with the coaches guiding us. I shared a special connection with them, and it was reciprocal. We sometimes went to other activities together, and they treated me like the daughter they never had. They had no children of their own.

I would occasionally arrive home to find my father in some drunken state, telling me that I didn't do something right or that he didn't like that I had argued with him about something, (usually around protecting my mother). As a punishment, he would prevent me from going bowling the following week.

Bowling was the only true pleasure I had! Feeling trapped in my own house, with increased frustration and resentment towards him, as well as a deep sense of loneliness and despair, I was always so glad to return to the bowling alley to see my friends, especially my coaches.

My father and mother came once to see me compete for a position on the travel team. He had been drinking and made a few snide comments with regard to even being there. I tried to ignore his comments and focused my attention on my competition. Deep in my heart, I was happy that they were there. However, I was also embarrassed by his commentary. Looking down the long alley at the two pins on one end of the lane and a single pin at the opposite end, I knew I had to make that last shot in the tenth frame in order to make the team. I cleared my mind, I focused, and I threw the ball down the alley. Thankfully, I was successful, in the clutch of the last frame and I was able to travel to a tournament in the US, without my family tagging along. A small sense of freedom!

From time to time my grandmother would sleep over at my house, and we would stay up late together. I always had a wonderful time with my grandma, talking, watching TV, laughing, and just being together as I intently listened to her stories. She was quite the night hawk. Often she would be found sleeping in her chair with a book on her chest. The TV would still be on, usually displaying the colour sequence or the Indian head on the screen, as the programming had ended for the evening. Oh, Canada could be heard playing in the background.

On one particular weekend, she was there, as my parents were away visiting relatives. I rose early Saturday morning in preparation for my bowling challenge and noticed that the TV was still on. The bed light was on in my parent's room, and my grandmother was sleeping soundly with a book on her chest. Suspecting that she had not been in bed that long, I chose to blow her a kiss on my departure rather than kissing her and possibly waking her. When I arrived home in the mid-afternoon, with excitement about my day at bowling, I noticed that the light was still on and my gran was still in bed. I entered the room to wake her and tell her about my day. I was looking forward to spending the remainder of the day with her, but was unable to wake her. Her hands were clutched to the blankets, and her body was stiff and cold. I realized that the only real friend I had in the world . . . was now gone!

I yelled her name and shook her, in hopes of waking her. Tears streamed down my face. She didn't awaken. At the funeral mass I told myself to keep it together as I didn't want anyone to comment on how 'she couldn't keep it together' or 'how she took it so hard.' As I stood by my grandmother's final resting place I was strong. Tears were not an option.

When I was in grade seven, I started getting visits from our landlord while my parents were out for the evening. He was a tall man, quite strong and persistent in his mannerism. Initially, he entered my house with a newspaper and said he wanted me to help him read. Instead, he proceeded to abuse me sexually. He fondled me, tried to penetrate me, and forced me to make him come. These were but a few of the sexual pleasures he enjoyed at my expense. During one of those encounters, it felt like my soul and spirit actually lifted from my body, and I simply disengaged. That activity persisted for an indefinite period of time. I kept it to myself, not knowing what would possibly happen if I ever told my parents.

I didn't share my experiences with anyone ~ no one to talk to. . . who would understand anyway? I remained silent.

Leaving home to attend University was a blessing in disguise. The alcoholic and abusive dysfunction in our home was replaced with a life of freedom and choice. A diverse and eclectic group of friends emerged through my studies and teaching fellowship. My attractions varied. I was going through some heavy questioning of myself and my attraction to both men and women. It truly became very challenging in my brain and my heart. In my reflection, I continued to struggle with my Catholic upbringing and wondering what choice was supposed to be right. The only thing that was really clear to me was that I loved deeply and with unwavering commitment.

Early in my studies at the University, I began hanging around with a group of gay women. I met this bright, youthful and engaging young woman who lived a short distance from campus. Time passed, and we became more serious in our relationship. We travelled together, both to her hometown and mine, meeting with family and friends. During those times, neither of us were able to celebrate our love and excitement about our lives openly with either of our families. Our union lasted for quite some time, until I was taken by complete surprise by a classmate who I never imagined would have had any interest in me.

Books were cracked open and a pencil dangled precariously from my ear as we flipped through the pages of our notes, preparing for our exam. A few classmates had gathered in my dorm room, and we were feverishly yelling out questions and answers to each other. As the evening progressed and minds overflowed with knowledge, people began to leave. One young woman lingered until after everyone, including my partner, had left for the evening. Perched against the pillows at the opposite end of the bed, she was fiddling with her notebook as I was packing up my books and clearing off the bed. She leaned over and kissed me on the lips. I instantly melted on the spot. I pushed the remaining books aside and laid beside her as we caressed, kissed and I became enraptured in her embrace. It felt like nothing I had ever experienced before or even imagined.

We continued to build our relationship, and at the end of the school term, we were elated by the news that we had both been accepted into the Master's Program as Teaching Fellows. We immediately made arrangements to move into an apartment to start our life together. We worked, played, and loved each other throughout the course of our studies, until an inexplicable distance suddenly occurred in our relationship. I was devastated when she suddenly began to spend a great deal of time with another student in our program - spending more time in her bedroom with this new person, than with me. My heart was broken. I cried for days, not understanding what had happened.

For years after that, relationships came and went. I didn't remain in any of them ~ always comparing and not letting go.

When University graduation was complete, I eventually returned to my home city and was fortunate to be hired as a teacher in my old high school. When the contract at that school finished, I found another teaching position in a school at the other end of the city. I quickly became involved with coaching and a variety of leadership activities. These roles gave me the opportunity to work with high school students in and out of class. I received an insight into their lives that I may not have had the privilege to share, had we only been in class together as teacher and student. It was a privilege that my bowling coaches had shared with me so many years ago. I now got to experience it from the other side!

Several students shared with me their background and struggles with their families, including alcoholism and violence. Some even questioned their lifestyle choices. Since I had experienced similar challenges, I was able to be more compassionate as I tried to guide them. I knew how important it was to be there to listen, and be the open heart of safety and security that they so greatly desired. I've learned that our past life experiences serve a purpose for our future. Mine have prepared me to be able to compassionately support students during difficult or confusing times in their lives.

Throughout my thirty years of being a teacher, coach, and principal in the school system, I have constantly seen the struggles that these students face. They worry about whether they will be accepted by their friends and families, whether their lives really matter or even whether they should take their lives. They wonder if they are loved and cared for.

So much of what they worry about is what I have also worried about - both in my youth and as an adult. During most of my professional life, I have been unable to be truthful and honest about my lifestyle. It didn't feel safe or secure to do so.

It has only been recently that I decided to take a stand for myself and for so many men, women, and children who are busy hiding. We have missed out for too long on experiencing unconditional love and having our spirit, mind, heart and soul genuinely celebrated for who we truly are. This needs to stop, and it begins with me. I can make a difference with the people whose lives I have the privilege to touch.

From now on, as I mentor and support people, I will be honest and truthful as I share the challenges and victories from my past. They happened for a reason. They serve a purpose. They can make a difference in helping people know that they are not alone. I will no longer be silent. I now have the courage to speak. By writing this story and sharing my past, I have chosen to stand in my truth.

For all of you who have been hiding in your life, this story is for you! Have the courage to speak and be heard.

About Elizabeth

Elizabeth Bennett is an award winning school principal, world traveller and running enthusiast.

She originally hails from Montreal, Quebec and has made her home in Calgary, Alberta with her beloved partner.

Her entrepreneurial spirit has led her to being a successful relationship marketing business owner, a certified advanced hypnotherapist, an accomplished student of NLP, and now a published author. Elizabeth is passionate about eliminating bullying with a purposeful focus on supporting and creating positive relationships with students, their families and the larger community of our broken world. She is grateful for the opportunity to convey her message with the intention of creating a space of courage for others to share their own stories and live with freedom and full self expression.

Joy, gratitude and love!

I am a brilliant woman because I empower people to live their best lives.

~ Elizabeth Bennett

I AM Audacious

From Fear to Fulfillment

By Jackie Maclean

I'm sitting in my lovely two-bedroom condo in Langley, B.C., counting my many blessings. It's a big job.

As a child, growing up in India with three siblings and my parents all packed into a two-room house, I never could have imagined such a life for myself. The journey from there to here has held heartbreak and disappointments – as well as great growth and immeasurable gifts.

The clues were there, if only I had the knowledge to recognize them.

We three girls did all the work at home. It was our job – never my brother's – to sweep the floor each night so we could unroll the sleeping mats. My mother was uneducated and timid, while my father was an angry alcoholic, unable to express love.

To him, life was a competition and he expected his children to do what he had been unable to accomplish.

I remember my father saying that girls are to go off and get married, and whatever he had to leave when he died would go to his son.

That made me angry – very angry. I remember making a promise to myself that whatever I had in the future would be shared equally among my kids, whether they were boys or girls. That was the first time I clearly remember vocalizing what became one of the tenets of my life: whatever I do, it has to be fair.

I was frustrated and angry with hand-me-downs, rationed food, our crowded house, filthy common toilets, my father's alcoholism and abuse, as well as sexual abuse by a tutor when I was a child. This anger would permeate my life for many years to come.

Dissatisfied at home, I welcomed the chance to get married at the age of nineteen. Unfortunately, my husband had much in common with my father, including alcohol and gambling addictions.

We moved to Dubai between the births of our two daughters so he could find better employment. It was a different world. I hadn't been happy in my old one and hoped for better opportunities there.

That life came to a crashing halt the day my husband suddenly died.

What could I do? I was a twenty-three-year-old widow with two toddlers. I refused to go back to my previous life. For a few months, I stayed with a cousin of my late husband. I ended up taking my daughters, who were aged ten months and two years nine months when their father died, to stay with his family in India while I worked two jobs in Dubai to support us.

I tried not to think about my daughters while I was away from them because it hurt too much. My life was an endless cycle of work-earn-sleep. Some people cope through addictions to smoking or drinking; I kept working. One thing I had gained was a strong work ethic, which served me well during this period of my life, in a culture that wasn't always tolerant of women in the workforce.

Only once a year, I could afford to go visit my girls. It broke my heart on one visit when my younger daughter pulled away when I reached for her. My in-laws didn't have a phone of their own for us to keep in touch or for the girls to even hear my voice from time to time, and I was a stranger to her.

After three-and-a-half years, I brought my daughters back to Dubai with me, before they got too settled into life in India. Their grandmother, aunts and uncle loved them dearly, but it was time for us to be a family again.

Eventually, I married my second husband and we had two sons. I'm glad to say that we never had 'step-this' or 'step-that' in our family; we were and are simply a family. What a blessing!

In the early 90's, we immigrated to Canada, settling in Langley, B.C. My husband got us established and then returned to his job in Dubai, visiting us two or three times per year and supporting us from a distance.

There were certainly challenges raising our family on my own in a new country. Our income was limited, as my husband supported both himself in Dubai and us in Canada. Because I believe in the importance of education, I sent our young sons to a private Catholic school. While it meant we would sacrifice some things, it was a matter of priorities.

My husband was a good salesperson and I was a good organizer, so we bought a printing business. We hoped that he could then move to Canada permanently and our family could be reunited.

The problem was that neither of us knew anything about printing. The equipment kept breaking down and there were always too many other things to pay before we could pay ourselves. With the business needing cash input, he returned to Dubai to live and work.

Frustrated by the situation, he left me for good. I couldn't understand why he had left. I was raised in a staunch Catholic home and divorce had not been part of my upbringing.

While my daughters had already left home, my sons were only thirteen and fourteen. Once again, I was a single mother. Beyond the emotional turmoil, I faced a frightening future with no solid source of income. It seemed to me that I had no future, which vaulted me into depression.

I remember finding a pair of shoes with holes in them that belonged to one of my boys. He hadn't told me because he knew we didn't have money for new ones. Essentially, we lived on canned tuna and a line of credit. I had no choice but to learn how to run a printing business, until I was able to sell it. Despite being able to sell it, I was still left with a huge accumulated debt that resulted in me filing for bankruptcy and losing my home to foreclosure.

To escape the worry that haunted me as we lived one hour to the next, I got involved in my community. That was a blessing in so many ways. I met more people and was able to give back to the community that had welcomed our family.

I was president of the local Rotary Club, a board member of various non-profits and earned my Distinguished Toastmaster accreditation. I was honored that our local Rotary twice awarded me its Paul Harris Award for community service that enhances the lives of others.

I founded an award-winning program through which volunteers donated, prepared and distributed thousands of sandwiches to homeless people in Vancouver's Downtown Eastside, Canada's poorest urban postal code. A few years ago, I passed on the leadership of 'Homeless on Hastings' to someone else. I'm pleased that it continues to provide food and other basics for Vancouver's neediest residents.

All of these activities helped me to look outside of myself and pulled me out of my worries, at least temporarily. However, I was still looking for a permanent solution to my unrest.

I found myself wanting to check out hypnosis as a path to healing. It was one of the best decisions I have ever made. Hypnosis changed my mindset and gave me more calmness in my life as I dealt with the business and raised my sons.

After I completed clinical hypnotherapy training, I saw some clients who seemed to make dramatic changes within only a few sessions. Some were quitting smoking in a single session while others regained their confidence and acquired a much desired job after a couple of sessions. Even I was amazed. How was this possible? I decided to dive in deeper. I re-did my training and started to get busy working as a certified hypnotherapist.

Hypnosis saved me. Learning to ask for help and taking the hypnosis course was my turning point. I am fortunate that I found the courage to rescue myself.

I named my business 'The Power Within' because I believe that through hypnosis, we really can access the incredible power that exists within each of us. I believe that creating a stronger, more resilient person (rather than simple symptom-removal suggestion) creates lasting change. I teach my clients techniques to empower themselves so they can change their lives for the better, just as I did. I inspire them and give them hope and the promise of a bright future.

Only permanent change gives clients the best chance to truly shift and be empowered, so that they can continue to grow and face future challenges on their own.

In my opinion, making a profit (on prescription drugs) has too often superseded the patient's best interests in our medical system. It has created a society where people have learned to expect a quick fix and too often stay stuck or even get worse.

My hope is that the tide is turning. I now receive an increasing number of referrals from physicians who realize that modern medicine often doesn't meet all of their patients' needs.

While I frequently hear "You're my last resort," my hope is that this type of work becomes the first resort for more and more people every day!

I love what I do because of the changes I witness in my clients. They learn to see themselves and their world in a different and more positive way, one that puts them in control of their lives.

Recently, I added Access Consciousness to my practice, which is a set of pragmatic tools that help individuals make changes quickly and dramatically in any and all areas of their lives. It has, once again, expanded my point of view of how life works.

As I continued, I gained additional understanding of my own life and how events surrounding it had influenced my thinking. My studies and my experience have taught me that we create our own reality, whether good or bad. I told myself that if I could create loads of crap in my life, I could change it, and change it I did! After years of telling myself I was born unlucky, my days are now filled with joy.

Part of what kept me from success was my unacknowledged belief, instilled during my childhood, that I wasn't worthy of it. I was trained to believe that I wasn't worthy of things until they were absolutely necessary. Now, I give myself the freedom to replace something before it wears out or breaks down!

Even though I grew up in a church-going household, I felt life was about survival and competition. My father envied others' success and tried – unhappily – to live his dreams through his children. Although he believed in education, he didn't know how to provide positive support to us.

Nobody taught them – or me – that we have the power within us to make real, positive change. Yet, there was always something in me that said my life didn't have to be that way. Who could I talk to about those feelings? I had questions and no answers.

When I took Law of Attraction training from Michael Losier, I learned that 'Selfish = Self-care.' I have now learned to make decisions based on my needs, not what other people expect or want me to do. Sometimes that means I don't fill a traditional role. Instead, I choose for myself and create a greater life, which allows me to give back fully to the people and world around me.

I frequently see the Law of Attraction at work in my life. If I have intentions to support and help other people, and put my needs out to the Universe, I know they will be met. These are small, subtle shifts in thinking, but they make such a difference in my life!

I have also come to realize that I am all about teaching – a deeper incarnation of the same instinct that had me volunteering in community organizations. I want to help other people in whatever way I can. Teaching is how I do that best, and I routinely offer coaching to business owners and corporate executives. I draw on my own experiences and training to help them move ahead and achieve more than they believed possible.

In my hypnosis practice, I teach people how to help themselves. Furthermore, I have taught self-hypnosis through Continuing Education and the local School District.

I especially enjoy helping those who are struggling with addictions or any destructive habit in their lives. Having lived so much of my life with addicts, I understand where they're coming from and what tragic results addiction can cause. My younger brother, who shared our father's addiction to alcohol, died when he was only thirty-six. Over the years, I have developed an addiction treatment method that gets consistent positive results.

Even though my life may seem like a long litany of losses – loss of my innocence to abuse, loss of my first husband to death, loss of well-paying jobs in Dubai that provided us with a luxurious lifestyle, loss of my second husband to divorce and the loss of my home to foreclosure – today I am at peace with where and who I am.

I am happy. I love my new home. I continue to enjoy many wonderful opportunities in my life. I am most proud of my amazing children, as they are now compassionate and practical adults. They understand the value of giving back and are very involved in family and their communities.

I see how my struggles have influenced them. They learned hard work from me and I encouraged them to obtain good educations. However, I also see that they believe that life requires endless hard work, because that is what they saw me doing as they were growing up.

I am trusting that they will also learn from the more recent changes I have made in my life, and gain their own peace. I can wish them nothing more valuable.

I love what I do and see my 'work' as play. I have the opportunity to travel and learn new ways of thinking while I experience new places and diverse people. I am creating a life of joy and freedom.

I've overcome many struggles to get here. In the process, I've learned that change – especially lasting change – is up to me. Once I fully accepted that I am worthy and have the strength within me to take control of my life, I was able to explore options to find what would work best for me.

Now, I find fulfillment by sharing what I've learned to help others overcome their own challenges. I tell them, if I could do it, so can you.

About Jackie

Jackie Maclean is a success coach and practicing hypnotherapist, certified by the International Medical and Dental Hypnotherapy Association and the National Guild of Hypnotists.

Her business is called, "The Power Within", because she has experienced herself how life-changing it is to recognize and nurture one's own internal power. She's devoted to helping others achieve fulfillment while finding peace and joy. She specializes in helping entrepreneurs and people dealing with any type of addiction.

As a volunteer for many organizations, Jackie has been recognized for her contributions to her community. She has four adult children, and lives in B.C.'s Fraser Valley.

Jackie can be contacted at www.thepowerwithin.ca

I am a brilliant woman because I make magic happen.

~Jackie Maclean

I AM Uninhibited

Who are You Being?

By Adora Nwofor

Have you ever put yourself last on the list, in a way that doesn't make your life your own? There have been many defining moments in my life and I am inspired to share one in particular with you. Stay with me right to the end. I promise it will be worth it. I am a comedian, so it has been a challenge to share something so crazy serious... but here it goes... on the other side of this story is my freedom to laugh at my life.

I have survived through abuse, violence, trauma and deciding who I would be under the microscope of a world that ousted me. One day I took all of that and became the person I am today. This is the story of how I became renewed and defined myself.

Black- Fade to thick fog, slowly disappearing.

I see lights heading towards me. I hear people screaming and recognize there is a group of people surrounding me. I think we are going to all get hit by a car if we do not move.

Just like a scene from a movie, I had lost consciousness and awoke to a surreal reality. I had been hit by a car. It finally registered and I was, as always, "okay". The first words out of my mouth were, "Can we just go in the restaurant? I'll clean myself up and we can carry on with your birthday dinner." I did not notice that my friend was crying. I didn't understand that I had landed on my face and neck after flying over the front of the car. 'Adora vs. Civic' is now a thing.

My first instinct: take care of everyone. While I was bleeding from several places, confused and in shock, I had already been through so many other things in my life that I knew I would be okay. I was at my peak. I was at my healthiest. My career was beginning to take off and I was anticipating a year that would make my dreams come true. This accident changed all that.

I was in the ambulance singing and making jokes, because that is what a comedian does when they are in trauma. "She has such a great attitude", "It's okay for you to be in the ambulance, you just got hit by a car" and "I think I hit her" were all things I heard.

I still had to process what had just happened. I didn't know what that looked like. I hadn't a clue how to stand up for myself.

Who was this person without strength? Strong was the norm for those around me. I was a professional at not putting myself on the list, in a way that made my life my own. So when and how does one make themselves a priority?

Yes I was strong. I was a single parent of three. I had overcome violence in my domestic life as a child and as an adult. Sexual assault is an experience that I am proud to say I have survived over and over again. I was well-versed in making all seem well for the benefit of proving myself right or someone else wrong.

This vehicle accident posed a new set of challenges. I had never had to fight my body on this scale, and it felt like the ultimate betrayal. I had a laundry list of injuries. My right hand was permanently damaged. I had a concussion that resulted in me being confused and clueless as to how to navigate the recovery process. Not only did I feel that my body betrayed me, but my mind also felt like it was not on my side.

What happened next? I was at the hospital for a few hours, left around 4 am and was in another city hosting an event by 6 pm. Upon reflecting on that day, I do not know how I made it through. I do know that it was not necessary for me to treat myself the way I did. "Show them you are dedicated and ensure you hide all that has occurred." I covered my facial injuries, wore a sweater to hide my arms and my dress was long enough that no one saw my legs. Why did I do that? I did it because there was no place for vulnerability in the life I had been living.

Within a week I was traveling for work to an awards show. I had to take my painkillers. "Pain changes you" is a statement that had been applied to my mental health, but never to my body in a way that impacted my mental health. I could not function as the outgoing, articulate, hardworking, detail-oriented and fun-loving person I knew. Within six months, I understood that nothing was the same anymore. What I had taken for granted was now a struggle. Cooking, cleaning, caring for my kids, working, writing and literally walking up the stairs was excruciating. Who was I? I didn't know this person. I was unfamiliar and uncomfortable with my life.

Without a family doctor, I found it difficult to get someone to take my health situation seriously. On the outside, I actually looked healthy and was technically functioning, but on the inside, I felt like I was fighting my body, my mind, society and the system. Initially, all I knew how to do was laugh. When I finally accepted that I was not well, I was crushed. I cried every day for three years due to the physical pain, emotional exhaustion and the fact that I was losing the care of my son. It was my choice to send him to his father. I just couldn't do it all, alone, anymore.

The child I fought so hard to have was no longer my friend. He couldn't understand what was happening to his 'super mom'.

The mom who had carried twins as a single woman, worked and gone to school full-time and then moved their home to create a better life for her family during the 8th month of her pregnancy. I had my twins at full term, with them weighing six and seven pounds. I lost the weight, had a corporate job and was thriving - then, *eerrch boom smash.* My son couldn't watch me suffer any longer, and I get it, but that was almost my demise. I was broken past my comprehension of being able to be fixed. My life as I knew it was over, again.

Lesson #1: Put yourself at the top of your list.

My soul did not give up. No matter how many tears I shed, or how much pain I was in, I went on. I had no clue what I was doing, yet I knew I had to do something. I went to work on my body. Physical Therapy saved me. A team of women helped to move my body and they told me I would be okay. They pushed me to my limit with stretches, workouts and IMS (Intramuscular Stimulation- that's when they put a needle into your muscle and interrupt it until it stops contracting, which is excruciating.) To get better, I had to put myself into more pain.

There was no empathy around me from my friends or family. I was told I was lazy and a liar. No one could see my physical or emotional pain and to them, it was non-existent. That reality was just as painful as everything else.

I kept moving forward blindly, and I began to recognize some things about myself. I always wanted to be better, and I know I can never be perfect. I don't know how to not keep learning to do more, strive more and do better. I didn't want to put off regaining my physical health. Being limited was getting in my way. The pain was so much to bare, but doing nothing to heal was not an option.

My mind would tell me that I was no longer able to work or volunteer, workout, do stand-up comedy, meal plan or empower women. Yet… all of these undone tasks were slowly being accomplished through my physio-treatments. I pushed hard, never revealing how much pain I was in. I took the worst job at night and could barely take care of my kids. I found out that I had PTSD (Post Traumatic Stress Disorder) which made me panic every time I got on the stage. The lights that were a part of my career reminded me of the lights that could have cost me my life. Yet I keep going back up there. I wanted to become the woman I knew before. I finally recognized how amazing she had been. A single mom who was doing her best to do everything. It was so much more than what I was able to do at that moment. I gave myself a long overdue break. I needed a revamp. That was the blessing of losing my 'hit by a car' virginity. It was my rebirth.

Despite three years of physical therapy, my pain levels had not changed as much as I had hoped. I knew it was time to do something different. I went home and actually rested. As I slowed down, I began to wonder if the pain would ever stop, if I kept pushing. I decided that it wouldn't. I had to do something radically different. I then realized that for my whole life, my perception of myself had been negative, low and demeaning - and that I was actually longing to once again be the 'less than' person I had fought not to be! It was a light bulb moment. That 'girl of old' was amazing and I wanted her back. I loved her and she deserved love. Every moment of her life, good or bad, perfect or flawed was amazing. I fell in love with myself! My eyes were open. I was still here. I was still standing. I now saw myself as a winner.

I believe everyone goes through life's challenges to wake themselves up. We cannot judge what others are going through, as we never know their pain and what they are overcoming to become who they are meant to be. I discovered I am incredible.

Lesson #2: What you have is valuable - work with it.

Our life experience is defined by those who touch our lives. My life had been touched many times by toxic people and events. I had never learned how to truly care about myself, my work and my looks or how I could give back. I only knew how to look after my own basic needs.

Recognizing that I had been a wonderful person was so empowering to me, yet it also made me feel lost. I didn't know how to heal myself. I was afraid that I would never get back to normal, and realized I would need to find a new normal. How does one do that? My mind began to consider new possibilities.

Through all this injury trauma, I kept pushing myself, even when I was supposed to rest. I never felt like my best was good enough. My house wasn't clean. I didn't have a job and I was struggling in life. Despite that, I pushed myself to love myself - flaws included. I accepted that I would not be the same and that I had to set new priorities, like being happy, rather than feeling depressed and suicidal. I could walk up the stairs and not feel like I had to pee. I could hug and love my kids. I could continue to be passionate about people, their stories and how they were shaped by them. I could talk to people about what was happening in my life and help them see what I saw. That reality had to be enough. It was all I had. I was determined to make it.

I began giving back to my community. It began with little things, like helping my neighbours and telling jokes that meant something to me. The more I spoke with people, the more I helped them to see me differently - and the more I began to see myself differently. My baby steps were now 'the steps of giants'. I had hit my rock bottom and was now climbing out of my hole. I didn't know it yet, but I would soon see the highest peaks! I was no longer taking ME for granted.

My reality was that I had gone over the top of a car, injured my body from neck to ankle and had injuries that no one could see. I had to trust myself again, because for a long time, I didn't. That was the biggest change in me. I host events and run for six hours in heels - smiling and dealing with anything that gets thrown in my direction with grace and empathy. No one knows that it takes me two days to recover. I had to be okay with that reality. I began to see that I'm just as good and capable as I was before. I just have to do things in a different way.

When your life is riddled with trauma, it can be difficult to see yourself outside of the hardship. In essence, one becomes the trauma and uses it as their definition. All my life I had been allowing my outside world to determine my worth. I was told I am 'too many to list' negative adjectives throughout my life. Toxic folk kept missing the mark. I will no longer give toxicity any more of my energy. Today's adjectives come from my reality and the people who can understand and empathize with the actuality of my own life. This is new to my consciousness and has changed everything again.

Lesson #3: Be positive.

Since expanding my own sense of worthiness, I have embraced the comedian that I am. I have been on stage telling jokes at festivals and as the host of festivals. I have co-hosted and produced a TV program, traveled the world, been in movies, met stars and made friends with stars. I give a voice to those who don't feel they are heard and make space for those who want to speak. I'm on boards to create change and I model designer clothing. Don't get me wrong, I still have moments where I either doubt myself or challenge my own definition of this person I have become. After all, I am now doing things that people told me I could never do.

I now believe that when we allow our experiences to define us, it is a disservice to our true selves. An experience can shape us and teach us, but is not the determining factor of our overall definition. It is so important to define who you are, despite what you are told about yourself during the journey. You alone know how and why you have become brilliant. Use this knowledge, as you become who you want to be. It's your decision.

My past experiences used to define and restrict me. Now I use them to remind myself that I am capable, brilliant and continuing to grow with each passing interaction. No matter what folks said about me, I made the choice to listen to my heart. I was and am good enough. No one knew my pain as a child, the secrets

I had to keep or the successes that were never acknowledged. My end game was always to have a goal that would make me something incredible. Now I know that no matter what – I am already incredible. I am proud because I now give myself permission to see the real Adora. None of my many accomplishments could have happened if I did not give my authentic, genuine Adora my full support. I love my life. I love the woman I AM.

About Adora

Adora Nwofor is unquestionable quality. She's certainly unique and yet has something relatable to every woman due to her anthropology background and plethora of extraordinary experiences.

Standing 6'1' she commands the stage as a comedian, model, and actor. She can be seen on stages hosting events such as Cariwest, femme wave, as well as the Grand marshal of the March for women (2017) where she hosted over 5000 women. Her comedy has a feminist pov with a dark twist that has been labeled by some as shock wit.

Her acting resume is slowly growing from local TV and Indy to reality to Nollywood and principle role such as *suck it up* (2016).

Modeling, styling and makeup are skills she uses to spread her message of body positivity, as seen in Avenue magazine's Best dressed list (Calgary 2017).

You can connect with Nora at adoranwofor.com

I am a brilliant woman because I am uninhibited. The world's adversity may slow me down but I remain unstoppable.

~ Adora Nwofor

I AM Perseverance

Awakening the Wisdom of My Soul

By Leticia Jones

I believe that painful experiences whether physical or emotional, can bring forth an awakening of who we truly are.

My story is about the challenges that occurred in my life that culminated in a crucial change after my husband died. That change gave me the opportunity to dive deeper into my practice of self-love and to appreciate my life more fully.

If you are a mom, I know you would agree that having children is challenging. My challenges started in the delivery room when I had my first baby. As I was giving birth there were major complications. I felt as if my life was slipping away as I saw a bright yellow light that surrounded the room. The light was beautiful and I realized it was a sign that everything would be okay. When I managed to turn my head to look at my baby boy, my heart was so full of gratitude. I couldn't stop looking at him and I prayed for the strength to keep fighting for my life and become healthy again.

My prayers were answered. Thankfully, two years later, I was able to give birth again to twin girls. Once again, the delivery process was difficult for both, yet those deep moments of physical pain and having my life at risk, have created an impact about how much I appreciate life and how important it is to fully live it.

Pain would enter my life once again. It was deep and emotional because my husband suddenly and unexpectedly passed away right in front of my eyes. In that moment, it felt like a part of me had died, as if my heart had broken into pieces. I was devastated and didn't know how I would move forward.

Two weeks before he passed away, I had a curious experience that perhaps was preparing me.

I was at the pool with my kids when a lady approached me and claimed she had a message for me. She told me that I was a great mom, commented on how wonderful my kids were and then told me that they were surrounded by angels that were looking after them. Then she referred to a man that had been in my life who was still looking after me and keeping me safe and that I needed to trust myself. We both felt that he was my grandfather, who passed years ago, and who I have always felt really close to. At the time, I had no idea why this stranger had approached me with that message.

In the years before my husband passed away, I had frequently struggled with bouts of depression. These episodes had kept me feeling stuck in life and I began to think that feeling depressed was somehow normal. In the moment that I saw my husband die, that suddenly began to change. It was as if a book of wisdom opened – bringing an abundant source of messages and information about what life really means.

I could clearly see how my big ego and the choices that I made throughout my life, led me on a path towards depression and not moving forward in life. I saw that little by little, my light had been turning off. I realized that being in the dark place of depression was one of the hardest challenges I ever faced in my life - and that it also contained a lesson that I needed to learn.

Facing the death of my husband brought me into a vulnerable place that required me to release self-judgement and to learn to love myself in a conscious way. As healing occurred, I found the strength to face my life, one day at a time. I eventually embraced the opportunity to learn more about my grieving and explore different areas of my life that I never paid attention to before.

Meditation and self-healing became a basic and necessary routine in my life. Thanks to this practice, I have been able to understand changes in my life from a different perspective. I learned that it is important to surround myself with a community of people that make me feel safe and that will provide me with help and support when I need it. I also learned to trust and follow my intuition. This led to discovering that the more I meditate, the more I connect to that gut feeling that gives me signals - even when I sometimes don't follow them. To me, that's intuition, and the more I trust it, the easier it is to make decisions.

When I went through the process of my husband passing away, it was very frightening. I wondered how I was going to do it all by myself - to look after my three kids, the finances, my job and my future. I worried that I would be alone forever! Now when fear comes, I recognized it as a black tunnel and feel confident that there is always a light at the end of it. I have learned that both good and bad experiences in life are temporary, and that it is simply a matter of time before things flow with ease.

Even when it feels like everything is lost, that nothing is going to make a difference or when I think that I am not good enough to do anything, I now remind myself that I always have the ability to choose what I want to do from a place of light and love. It seems that the crashing moments in life come to help us to move forward and to unfold how wonderful and powerful we actually are. By choosing to consciously create my own inner world and giving myself permission to trust, things in my life began to change.

I started to be more selective about how and who I spent my time, as I now recognized how valuable a gift it is. I became more careful as I learned that time is *love*. When I love myself, I use my time wisely with the people, activities and things that are the most important in my life.

A lot of intense and special moments have happened that have given me support during my process of grief, fear, falling apart, breaking into pieces and putting myself back together again. I have gone through the process of self-discovery and become aware of how life has given me the opportunity to start all over again. The death of one of the most important people in my life taught me to appreciate life. I have moved from feeling confused and wondering why my husband needed to die, to understanding that a divine source heard the voices of his heart and they knew it was his time. He had such a kind heart and generous soul and deserved to receive many blessings. My relationship with my husband now feels even closer - full of harmony, peace and love. I can even occasionally feel his presence and his energy throughout my body, and I know he is now guiding me and watching over me and our kids.

Over the years, many different angels have come to help me and my three kids. One that has fulfilled my life on so many levels, was a particular lady at my workplace. Something felt right to go to her and start a conversation. We discovered that we had very similar life paths and backgrounds. I learned that her husband had passed away in the same month and year as mine. In fact, he passed away within nine days of when my husband passed away. I was quite shocked to hear that! Both men carried the same name and their birthdays were only ten days apart. How can you explain that one? We became instant friends, and as we hugged, a very memorable song started to play on the radio. It was very special. Later on, she came to visit and have dinner with me and my kids. She was quite surprised when I served the meal I had prepared, saying, "This is the last meal I had with my husband". It almost feels like our husbands planned for us to meet. We have become a great support for each other as we understand life from the same perspective.

I continued to receive constant messages through dreams, books, nature, music, meditation and people who showed up in my life. They have all helped me to think of and follow the right direction at the time. They have also helped me to learn how to separate my physical body from my soul, so that I can do my daily activities and face my every day life while also letting my heart and spiritual being heal on a higher level. It doesn't mean that all is healed and resolved, but I feel like I have survived a major moment of my life.

People often ask me how I am able to keep myself on my two feet and live my life the way I do. When they see me laughing, dressing up in colourful clothes, saying jokes or being silly, they sometimes ask me how I manage to look so good, and be moving forward in my life. It doesn't seem to make any sense to them. My answer is that I have decided to see my cup as being half full, not half empty. My inner voice told me, "Don't expect anybody to understand because nobody is in your shoes, only you are. Follow your heart, your intuition and trust that your decisions are made from the knowledge and wisdom that comes from your very own life experiences". As I awaken from each stage of my grieving, I ask myself, "Why not? Why keep denying who I am, my talents, my opportunities and my mission in this life?" My husband has given me a very clear message about how precious life is and the importance of loving myself. He wants me to continue living a happy and healthy life, to show gratitude and to take the opportunities that life is presenting every single day.

Thanks to my spiritual and natural healing path, I have been able to go deeper and find myself in a place where I can speak with truth as I face who I really am and what I really want in life. When I ask myself, "What am I waiting for?" a soft voice reminded me to simply trust, rather than being afraid and doubtful. I have received divine guidance to start fresh and create a new beginning that speaks to my heart. As I do that, I can also teach my kids how to overcome a difficult time with love, integrity, respect, perseverance, temperance and faith. I have learned to be open to miracles, as they really happen when we are ready to receive them.

There is no manual when it comes to grieving the loss of a loved one, however; I will share with you a few of my practices during my journey.

1. **Have support around you**. Keep yourself in a place where you feel safe emotionally, mentally, physically and spiritually. Having a positive and supportive group of people around you is so important.

2. **Be thankful.** Count all the positive things around you, even when it is as simple as waking up and being able to get out of bed. Appreciation and being thankful attracts more abundance and support in your life.

3. **Travel in time.** Remember those special moments and memories of family, friends, places, food or music. Those moments help you reconnect to who you are, what

direction you want to take in your life, and to give yourself the chance to start all over again.

4. **Go deeper in your healing**. Your present wounds, feelings and emotions are most likely connected to old experiences. This is a great time to let go from the root and free your heart and soul.

5. **Connect to Source.** On the days you feel overwhelmed connect to your Source. This may be God, Nature or simply a moment of silence. Focus on what really matters to you and what you need for your own process of growth and transformation. It takes a lot of energy and courage to be strong and to set your limits. Be gentle and be patient with yourself. This can be an enjoyable journey.

6. **Keep moving forward no matter what**. On your journey you may fall down many times. What is important is getting back up. It is okay to be vulnerable and to recognize and let go of what does not serve you any more. Say yes to life and the new opportunities. Things eventually will unfold in the right direction. Open your heart to new opportunities, as they will show up in many ways.

7. **Write in a journal.** Express your emotions and experiences as you move through your healing process. It will help you put things in perspective and to discover new things about yourself and how much you deserve to be happy!

8. **Love yourself unconditionally.** Let go of any type of self-judgment, as it will only limit your self-growth and healing. Remember that no one else knows you better than you know yourself. Loving yourself will also bring loving, caring and helpful people into your life.

We have been given a physical body with all its limitations, however; when we work on a deeper level we can find out who we truly are. My kids have taught me about resilience and how there is not a final goal in the journey. We all now live every day with the gifts that life has to offer. I have learned in rendering service to others by living soul-fully, truth-fully and heart-fully. When I do, miracles show up.

I encourage you to be open to receive the gifts and messages that life has for you, and to connect with the light that is always there for you! Everything around you becomes a mirror that reflects who you are and what needs to heal. Pay attention to it.

Decide everyday where you want your soul to be - from the moment you open your eyes until you close them at night. Take time to be with yourself, in silence, to connect with your core. Touch your heart with your hands and hear it's messages as it beats. Sit in a quiet place and have a conversation with your body. What does it say? What do you need to change? Who do you need to forgive? What do you need to let go of? Talk to your soul, connect with your 'source', and remember that you are never alone!

About Leticia

Leticia D. Jones was born in Mexico. She has a Bachelor of Business Administration and Human Resources degree. Over the years she became more aware of Natural Healing, experiencing different modalities about how to treat herself.

Leticia is owner of Temazcal Natural Self-Healing and Founder of Mujer y Salud (Women and Health). Offering to the Hispanic woman the opportunity to grow, connect and heal through holistic services such as workshops, retreats, classes and personal coaching in Spanish. Expanding her services to other countries such as Mexico.

Inspired by her children, she also developed a program for Children, "Play & Connect", teaching meditation, breathing exercises and brain-body movements. It is important for her to be able to teach these tools for life to children so they grow healthy and happy.

Her mission is to use her experience and knowledge to offer an effective natural alternative to help others heal their body, mind and spirit.

Her goal is to help you to develop a better relationship with yourself, so you enjoy life to its fullest, feeling happier and healthier.

Connect with Leticia at www.temazcal.ca

I am a brilliant woman because I transformed my painful experiences into a tree of wisdom and freedom

~Leticia D. Jones

I AM Compassionate

Learning to Fly

By Shauna Walker

"Look if you had one shot or one opportunity to seize everything you ever wanted, in one moment would you capture it or just let it slip?"

Eminem, "Lose Yourself"

The songs I quote throughout this story were my 'voice' when I felt I didn't have one. In the times of my life when it was very difficult for me to pick myself up and continue, I always found solace in the words of these songs. My 'out', was to run to my room, turn on the music, crank the volume up to it's maximum, and create my sanctuary, my safe place to land. When I shut everything else out to survive, my music and the words I heard provided me with a sense that I wasn't alone. I didn't feel so empty or isolated in my pain. These words gave me the strength to carry on and motivated me when I had nothing else to inspire me. Music has always held me in a gentle way. It's been the healing of my soul, and through the words of songs that have resonated with me I felt in a strange way that someone else out there could also feel my pain. Music has inspired me to be in forgiveness, and in my heart I accept that gift.

It has taken me a long time to find my voice. When a child feels unseen, frightened, traumatized and never validated in a good way……they lose their voice. That was true for me. Who do we turn to? Who do we talk to? Who do we tell? Losing my voice was not something I consciously knew I had done. As a young adult, I eventually left home and adjusted to the world as best I could. As I became successful, I found 'my voice' - but was it really my voice? It was not the authentic one that sat inside me, bursting at the seams to be heard. My stomachs churns as I write this and I feel a little (actually a lot) insecure and self conscious, but deep down in my soul I know my story is important.

There are many levels of abuse and I can only hope that my story will connect with those who have experienced a similar childhood. We are not so alone after all. When we share our stories with each other, it is empowering and relieving. I have now found a place to belong, in a way I had never felt before. I was raised Catholic and see now how those old beliefs kept me stuck in a confused way. Deep down in my soul I always had a sense of knowing that these teachings, this mindset of fear and secrets, just didn't sit well with me. Who would I betray if I denied it? Would something bad happen to me or perhaps someone close? Something 'bad' had already happened, and no one talked about it.

Everyone had lost their voices.

In our world today we have come a long way. The days of being beaten down and having nowhere to turn have changed. The women who came before us, who fought so hard and so selflessly to make a better world for all of us, need to be honoured for all they gave so that their suffering wasn't in vain. I saw an article recently where a woman named, "Dorothy Day" was standing holding up her prison dress. It was in 1917. Day went to prison for being one of forty women in front of the White House protesting women's exclusion from the electorate. We never want to go back to that dark time in history. Today we have to stick together; we have to honour the strong women we come from. To spend our time blaming, criticizing and excluding is empty and valueless. It's time to step up and rise above this. When we do, doors open and people arrive in our lives to guide us through our fears and insecurities. In short, miracles happen. I'm just like you. I had to find my way and I know you will find yours. My voice is in my story and now I am ready to tell it.

The Early Years

I was never a victim; I've always been a fighter. Not in an angry way, but perhaps coming from a sense of something pulling me forward in a way I did not yet understand.

I never could own the emotions I felt coming from what we label as abusive. I didn't know any better and felt I had a normal and happy life… didn't I? At a deeper level, I had been damaged in some way but I was too young to know differently, too little to understand.

How could I understand the pain my father endured, which led to abuse in various forms and would ultimately affect my childhood? I was always there for my siblings, nurturing and supporting them. I was especially always there for my Mother. Through the eyes of a child and in my innocence, I felt her pain when she was mentally and physically beaten down, and feeling exhausted and unsupported. Without the tools I have now, I took on the role of being her protector. This is what a child does from a bond of love. It is too much for any child. No one asked or expected me to do it. I just wanted everything to be better, so I stepped into much more than I could handle. What I really needed, was to find a place to belong, to be normal and mostly, to feel seen and loved.

The Adolescent Years

I would listen to the following song over and over again. It spoke deeply to me and still does.

I don't want to start

Any blasphemous rumours

But I think that God's

Got a sick sense of humour

And when I die

I expect to find Him laughing

Depeche Mode, "Blasphemous Rumours"

I left home at eighteen to make my way in the world. In order to escape my pain, I ran. I was numb, couldn't face reality and really just existed with a deep knowing that I would come through it. Did I know how? No.

What was I running from? I didn't know. Was I still held back with strong feelings of guilt that I had abandoned my siblings, my Mother, my home? I don't know. All I knew was that this was my normal. How was I supposed to know how to act or feel, through all this numbness and pain? Yet… somehow I managed. In time, slowly, with separation and life experience, I was able to see the future a little differently. Life seemed to settle down and I started to fall into a whole new pattern. All the while, I was still in an existence of numbness that I was totally unaware of.

Finding My Voice

The start of my healing began when I married my husband. It continued with the birth of my two amazing children. As I watch them grown into the beautiful souls that they are, I am supported in trusting that I am enough, I am feeling peaceful and I am now happy.

When my daughter was born, being part of that life force was overwhelming and terrifying. It was also one of the greatest gifts in my life. She continues to be my inspiration every day. My son was born 5 years later and once again I felt so much love. I had so much to look forward to. I was determined to protect my children in a way that I never was.

Being a Mother had brought me so much joy and healing, but my journey was yet to begin. It looked like I had it all. In many ways I did, and yet I still felt something was missing. I still had no voice and this was holding me back from stepping fully into myself. I didn't feel seen, heard or that I belonged. I still felt guilty about everything. How could I set myself free from this burden?

What I've felt, what I've known

Never shined through in what I've shown

Never be

Never see

Won't see what might have been

What I've felt

What I've known

Never shined thought in what I've shown.

Never free

Never me

So I dub thee unforgiven

Metallica, "The Unforgiven"

The Healing Years

I have always believed there was something 'more' that I just hadn't connected with yet. I could sense it and trusted my own intuition to guide me. When we are ready to step into that 'knowing', it's frightening. It is a new beginning that cannot happen without change occurring in all aspects of our life. That change is what scares us the most. Stepping into a piece of myself I had never seen or experienced was daunting. I knew that if I didn't step through that fear, there would be no change or forward movement. My story would remain the same. In the end it is just that, a story. I had to find a way to heal that small, frightened and confused child within, who never had the support, knowledge or tools to understand what all the pain in her system was. Who was I?

Time marched by, I existed, and I convinced myself that I was healed. I had found a good partner; I was not being beaten; I was being provided for in a good way; I had beautiful healthy children; a good job; I was loved. I was doing all the right things, wasn't I? How could I know? I had no normal to gauge this on.

At a deep level, my soul knew. It longed to be seen as it's authentic self and to rise to the surface, clean, whole and complete. To belong, to have a voice, but mostly to believe that I had something important to say. Some things we cannot explain. Deep in my soul, something started to niggle and feel unsettled. When I had moments of anxiety, uncertainty or fear, I would hear it begging to shout out to the world to see me.

As a mother of two small children, I knew I had to break this pattern. I wasn't even sure what pattern I had to break or what I had to fix. After all, hadn't my childhood been "normal"? Where was I to start? How was I going to do this? Who would I trust? Could I trust? As I watched my children accept me in complete and unconditional love, I knew I had to find a way to be able to open up and give all of that and more back to them. They were and still are my greatest inspiration and my most gentle of healers.

Five years ago, a good friend and colleague stumbled upon a form of therapy which she encouraged me to go check out. It had changed her whole process of looking at her own issues. I had already felt the pull towards something I couldn't define, and when this work was mentioned to me it felt right. I decided to explore it further and I can honestly say that was the best gift I could have given myself. It has totally changed my life. This work is called, "Family & Systemic Constellations". It has nothing to do with the stars, but everything to do with empowering people to step out of family entanglements that have kept them stuck in repeated patterns that they are often unaware of. Like the tangled roots of a tree, we are born into what came before. Constellations provide us with a new lens to look at what we are carrying, that never belonged to us in the first place. Our ancestral roots run deep and we carry so much baggage - all from a bond of love. Until these hidden dynamics are revealed and we get to see a clear picture of who or what we are entangled with, we can never be free from the experiences of our past.

This work provided me with tools to step out of my story and feel the truth of these experiences in my physical body. I now see my life through a whole new lens. I had started to find my voice and I finally found myself belonging, included and knowing I had something important to say. I had begun a beautiful journey of releasing a story that no longer belonged to me. I could now see through compassionate eyes, a gentle and forgiving heart and I knew I had found my way back to me. Everything had changed.

Today I love who I have become. I hold my family close and am filled with so much gratitude for the lessons, the strength and all the gifts I have taken from this experience. I have heard the words, "The best revenge is success". Today I now choose to use my voice in a positive and clear way as I inspire others to know they too can find a way through when they are ready. My voice gets stronger every day and every year. I look forward to where it will lead me as I step into a whole new sense of self. I sit in my brilliance. I embrace it. It is my greatest joy to share who I am with all the beautiful, strong and brilliant women in my life.

Today I am proud to say, I am a successful business owner. My passion is to empower others who have also walked in my shoes. When we learn to love ourselves, we find more compassion, more understanding and yes, more love. We do this by feeling supported and safe in an environment that enfolds us, sees us for who we are, without judgment, criticism or an agenda. I do this in my business through offering a "Spa Ritual" to my clients. It honours and respects each guest, on their personal path to rejuvenation. We need to be gentler with ourselves, to receive more pleasure, more joy and mostly, more love in our lives.

I want women everywhere to know that they too can aspire to remember who they are, embrace their own brilliance and achieve their dreams. Reach out and share your stories, find your voice and feel safe in the embrace of others who understand. Together we can change the world. We really can build mountains. We have always been the keepers of the earth. Together we are amazing.

Instead of blaming, pointing fingers and staying with the pain of being stuck, I now embrace the strength and love I got from my parents, my siblings, my grandparents and all the lessons I have learned along the way. I embrace how strong I have become because of it all. I can do the rest myself now. My story has changed. I now know that my parents gave me all they could, and perhaps more than they got. I now understand that whatever happened with them was continued through me, and until I was able to let it go, the pattern would repeat. I love and embrace the strong woman I have become, the joy in my days and the love in my heart. Today I have learned how to fly.

Well some say life will beat you down

Break your heart, steal your crown

So I've started out for God knows where

I guess I'll know when I get there

Tom Petty, "Learning To Fly"

About Shauna

Shauna Walker, an avid spa goer and owner of The Spa Ritual, is passionate about the guest experience and is an advocate for healthy lifestyles.

The culmination of Shauna's vision is the creation of a refined spa experience, at The Spa Ritual in NW Calgary. This quality day spa was inspired by the gracious hospitality experienced during her travels to South East Asia.

Shauna has instilled her passions into her creation, carefully cultivating programs, which honors and respects each guest, inviting him or her on a person path to rejuvenation.

As Spa's director, Shauna mentors and inspires her team of professionals to make a difference in the life of each guest – by planting a tiny seed of self-rejuvenation as the cornerstone to wellness during every spa experience.

Following lessons learned from her own life experiences, Shauna deeply believes in the vital need of "taking time out" to reset and renew the process of our bodies and minds.

Shauna can be contacted at www.thesparitual.com

I'm a brilliant woman because I love the woman I have become.

~ Shauna Walker

I AM Gratitude

About Women Embracing Brilliance

Women Embracing Brilliance was created to support, encourage and celebrate women who are committed to find their voice, reclaim their feminine power and embrace the highest version of who they are – *their Brilliant Self.*

Our vision over the next five years is to positively impact the lives of women around the world, by empowering them to embrace and stand in their boldness, brilliance and beauty.

How? When one woman embraces her brilliance, her *soul signature* radiates out through her own voice of love, compassion and encouragement, which plants a seed in those around her. That seed becomes a ripple effect igniting the light within others and contributing to the evolution of humanity.

We are a global community of heart centered women who are dedicated to making a difference by empowering each other to live in optimal health, love and prosperity. As we embrace and ignite our brilliance we create heaven on earth for all.

For more information about WEB or to become a member visit:
www.womenembracingbrilliance.com

If you have a story that you are ready to share, and would love to be a contributing author in Volume Three of:

I AM a Brilliant Woman

contact Karen Klassen karen@karenklassen.ca

Suggested Reading

The Tipping Point – Malcom Gladwell

A New Earth – Eckhart Tolle

Why Walk When You Can Fly – Isha Judd

Rising Strong – Brene Brown

Living in the Freedom Frequency – Karen Klassen

The Gifts of Perfection – Brene Brown

You Can Heal Your Life – Louise Hay

Prosperity Consciousness – Chutisa and Steve Bowman

71748813R00079

Made in the USA
Columbia, SC
08 June 2017